More Make -n- Takes
for
Phonology and Literacy

Eight Reproducible Storybooks with Articulation & Language Activities

Christi Gansen
Edward Gansen

Super Duper® Publications • Greenville, South Carolina

10   09   08   8   7   6   5   4

Library of Congress Cataloging-in-Publication Data

Gansen, Christi, date
      More make-n-takes: 8 Reproducible Storybooks with Articulation & Language Activities / Christi Gansen, Edward Gansen.
           p. cm.
      Includes bibliographical references.
      ISBN 1-932054-08-1 (pbk.)
      1. Reading—Phonetic method. 2. Reading (Early childhood)—Activity programs. I. Gansen, Edward, date-II. Title.

LB1573.3.G364 2003
372.46'5—dc21

                                2003055276

Printed in USA

Illustrations by Edward Gansen
Cover design by Debbie Olson

Trademarks: All brand names and product names used in this book are tradenames, service marks, trademarks, or registered trademarks of their respective owners.

Super Duper® Publications
Post Office Box 24997 • Greenville, South Carolina 29616 USA
www.superduperinc.com
Call 1-800-277-8737 • Fax 1-800-978-7379

For our parents,
who supported and inspired us throughout our education.

About the Authors

Christi Gansen is a speech-language pathologist with the Edgerton School District in Edgerton, Wisconsin, where she has worked with preschool and early elementary students for the past 14 years. She holds a Master of Arts degree in Communication Disorders from the University of Northern Iowa and the Certificate of Clinical Competence in Speech-Language Pathology from the American Speech-Language-Hearing Association.

Edward Gansen is a freelance graphic designer and illustrator. He holds a Master of Arts degree in Advertising Design from Syracuse University.

Contents

Preface

More Make-n-Takes for Phonology and Literacy is a continuation of the project that developed as a result of my frustration with a lack of appropriate, literacy-based materials to target multiple speech and language goals. I wanted materials that would facilitate expressive phonology skills, provide children with engaging literacy experiences, and be time-efficient. Many of the children on my speech-language caseload needed intense phonological training, as well as language intervention. Finding the time in their schedule to do both separately and consistently was always a challenge. Incorporating stories into phonology training addressed this need, but it was difficult to find engaging stories that would facilitate production of target sounds. Some intervention materials were available with stories written to target specific sounds or phonological patterns, but the stories were often short and did not seem to offer much utility for language or literacy development. Other resources identified popular children's books that contained specific sounds, but it was difficult to determine if sound patterns would occur frequently enough in the stories for them to be worthwhile for intervention. Again, time was an issue—time to find the specific book, time to determine frequency of occurrence of target sounds, time to become familiar with the story line, and time to devise activities related to the story that would reinforce target sound productions.

Ed and I decided to create our own storybooks with rhyming and fanciful story lines that appeal to young listeners and the adults who read and work with them. We began with three stories to address final /s/ clusters, a common need with my students. Discussions with Linda Schreiber at Thinking Publications prompted expansion of the series to address all the primary phonological targets recommended by Hodson, Scherz, and Strattman (2002). As the story lines developed, it seemed natural to link other language and literacy activities to the themes so they could be used by educators or specialists for instruction or remediation. The two-volume series of *Make-n-Takes* and *More Make-n-Takes* provides storybooks and activities for clinicians and teachers to promote sound awareness, sound pattern acquisition, early literacy, and language skills in a time-efficient and fun way.

Acknowledgments

Our deepest appreciation goes to the many people who have inspired and supported us in the development of these materials. Special thanks go to Christi's colleagues in the Edgerton School District, who offer endless encouragement and are always open to new ideas, especially Judy Heil, Suzanne Granger, and Sharee Witt, for trying early versions of the *Make-n-Takes* series with students and sharing feedback as we developed the materials. We want to thank the students and staff of Edgerton Community Elementary School in Edgerton, Wisconsin, and Adams Elementary School in Janesville, Wisconsin, for being enthusiastic audiences to early versions of our stories. We also appreciate the enthusiasm and efforts of the staff at Thinking Publications—Linda Schreiber, Joyce Olson, Debbie Olson, and Sarah Thurs. Finally, we wish to thank Rae Cuda, Linda Fitzgerald, Janet McCauley, and Jackie Reeder for their time and efforts reviewing the project in its final stages.

Introduction

Overview

More Make-n-Takes for Phonology and Literacy is the second release in the *Make-n-Takes* series, especially designed to target the primary sound patterns in the cycles phonological remediation approach (Hodson, 1997, 2000; Hodson, Scherz, and Strattman, 2002). *More Make-n-Takes* contains eight stories that target the following patterns for ages 3–9 years:

- Syllableness (two and three syllables)
- Initial consonants (/p, m, w/)
- Final consonants (/m, n, p, t/)

- Final velars (/k/)
- Initial velars (/k, g/)
- Initial glottals (/h/)

The eight stories in the companion resource book, *Make-n-Takes* (Gansen and Gansen, 2003), target initial anteriors, initial and final /s/ clusters, and liquids. Either resource book in the series may be used separately, or both may be used to target all primary target patterns. Each of the eight units in each resource book contains a list of the words and speech sounds targeted in the storybook, so users may individualize their story selection based on the needs of each child.

The units contain all the needed materials: the storybook, sequence cards, picture cards, word count lists, picture card lists, production practice and carryover activities, and extension activities. Appendix A provides a summary of the target phonemes and patterns in each story, as well as other language skills that may be targeted in intervention. Black-and-white storybooks, sequence cards, and picture cards may be photocopied from this book (pages are perforated for easy removal, if desired) or they may be printed from the accompanying CD-ROM: *More Make-n-Takes Software Companion*. Full-color versions of the storybooks and sequence cards may also be printed from the CD-ROM. Instructions for creating full-size and child-size storybooks are contained in Appendix B and in the Table of Contents file on the CD-ROM.

Target Audience

The *Make-n-Takes* series is appropriate for children from 3–9 years of age. The materials may be used by speech-language pathologists to facilitate speech production using a phonological process approach or traditional articulation remediation. The materials may also be used by general and special educators to develop receptive and expressive language, cognitive concepts, and early literacy skills, including phonological awareness and concepts of print.

Goals

More Make-n-Takes for Phonology and Literacy supports the development of children's expressive and receptive language and early literacy skills. Each unit may be used to target these goals:

- Increase speech intelligibility
- Increase perception and production of target phonological patterns or speech sounds
- Use target language features in the context of a story (See Appendix A for a list of possible language targets.)
- Increase early literacy skills, including phonological awareness and concepts of print

Background

According to Hodson and Paden (1991), a vital component of phonological remediation is providing opportunities to practice sound patterns in controlled activities that are natural and meaningful to a child. Ideally, children with expressive phonological delays are identified during the preschool years, a time when it is also important for them to be exposed to numerous literacy experiences (Burns, Griffin, and Snow, 1999). Since reading stories is a common activity for preschool and school-aged children, incorporating stories in phonological sessions provides natural and meaningful contexts to hear and practice sound patterns and to begin building early literacy skills.

The concept of using story formats in phonological remediation is not new. Resources are available that identify which popular children's books contain specific sounds. Some include sound-specific word lists, but do not necessarily give an exact count of the number of times the words occur in the stories; others provide a total count of the words but do not delineate the count according to word position or blend combinations (e.g., final /ps/ or final /ks/). Without complete word count information, it is difficult to determine if sound patterns will occur frequently enough for the story to be worthwhile for phonological remediation. Some intervention materials have been written for specific phonemes or target patterns. While these stories have a high frequency of the target phonemes or patterns, their content is generally limited to a short story that has little application for literacy learning. The story lines themselves are not designed to readily lead children to acquire other academic or critical thinking skills.

More Make-n-Takes: 8 Great Storybooks for Sound & Language Play was developed to merge the goals of phonological remediation with rich literary experiences. The stories incorporate a high concentration of words containing a target phonological pattern in progressive, rhyming story lines. The format provides opportunities for listening to (i.e., auditory bombardment) and speaking the target pattern while exposing children to another level of phonological awareness through rhyming. From an academic and literacy perspective, the stories facilitate sequencing, oral storytelling, narrative structure, critical thinking skills, and number concepts. Extension activities related to each story are provided to address these areas. Activities can be implemented in remediation sessions, the classroom, or at home. Clinicians can consult with teachers and parents regarding the goals of the remediation program and how to use activities or techniques that will facilitate carryover of learning to other settings.

Before You Begin...

Before beginning intervention, administer a formal articulation or phonological assessment, such as *The Assessment of Phonological Processes–Revised* (Hodson, 1986). This will provide baseline information for setting goals and measuring progress. Traditional articulation tests will identify specific phonemes to address, while a phonological process analysis will identify the child's error processes and the phonological patterns that need to be developed to increase intelligibility.

According to Hodson and Paden's (1991) approach, a phonological process analysis is used to measure the frequency of error processes before beginning intervention and again after each phonological cycle to measure progress. Children produce words during interactions with specific objects, and their productions are transcribed according to the types of phonological processes the child uses. Percentages of occurrence are computed for the various deviant processes, and a level of severity for phonological delays is determined. When a child is identified as having a significant phonological delay, Hodson et al. (2002) offer several suggestions for determining which patterns to target and in what order (see Figure 1, page 4). Intervention is structured in phonological cycles, during which each target phonological pattern is addressed in succession.

Analyze the assessment information and plan which phonological patterns to target in a cycle. Sixty minutes per target sound within a pattern is recommended. Once targets are identified, individual sessions can be planned.

Figure 1

Potential Target Patterns

Primary Potential Target Patterns

(For beginning cycles; target only those that are consistently deficient *and* stimulable.)

Early Developing Patterns

Syllableness
(Utterances restricted to monosyllables)
Target: Vowel sequences in compound words
2-syllable; 3-syllable

C̲V̲ (If producing only V or VC or a class of
early developing C [stops, nasals, glides] deficient)
Typical target: Initial labial(s)

V̲C̲ (If final C lacking)
Targets: Voiceless stops (final
/p/, /t/, /k/, and/or final
/m/ or /n/ if lacking)

Anterior/Posterior Contrasts

Posterior obstruents (If lacking velars/glottal)
Target(s): (Depending on whether deficient and if stimulable)
Final /k/, then initial /k/, /g/, and/or /h/

Anterior (If evidencing of backing)
Target(s): Alveolar stops
Final /t/; initial /t/, /d/ (possibly /n/)

/s/ Clusters

Word-initial /sp, st, sm, sn, sk/ (Depending on stimulability)

Word-final /ts, ps, ks/

Liquids

Word-initial /l/ (Preceded by a week of tongue-tip clicking)
Possibly /l/ clusters

Word-initial /r/ (Suppress gliding process)
Possibly /r/ clusters

(Reassess and recycle patterns as needed before progressing to Secondary Target Patterns.)

....

Secondary Potential Target Patterns

(After establishment of early developing patterns, contrastive use of velars/alveolars, /s/ cluster emergence in conversation,
and suppression of gliding while producing liquids in carefully selected production-practice words, progress to
secondary patterns that remain problematic; incorporate minimal pairs whenever possible.)

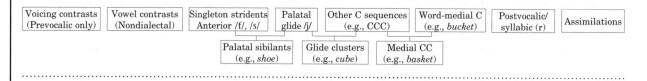

Voicing contrasts
(Prevocalic only)

Vowel contrasts
(Nondialectal)

Singleton stridents
Anterior /f/, /s/

Palatal
glide /j/

Other C sequences
(e.g., CCC)

Word-medial C
(e.g., *bucket*)

Postvocalic/
syllabic (r)

Assimilations

Palatal sibilants
(e.g., *shoe*)

Glide clusters
(e.g., *cube*)

Medial CC
(e.g., *basket*)

....

Advanced Potential Target Patterns

(For upper-elementary-grade-level children with intelligibility problems.)

Complex consonant sequences
(e.g., *extra*)

Multisyllabicity
(e.g., *unanimous*)

From "Evaluating Communicative Abilities of a Highly Unintelligible Preschooler," by B.W. Hodson, J.A. Scherz, and K.H. Strattman, 2002, *American Journal of Speech-Language Pathology, 11*, p. 240. © 2002 by the American Speech-Language-Hearing Association. Reprinted with permission.

Using *More Make-n-Takes* for Phonological Remediation

Overview of Materials

Each of the eight units in this resource book includes a black-and-white storybook, corresponding sequence cards, picture cards (i.e., reproducible black-and-white line drawings of target words), a list of words from the story that use the target pattern with frequency of occurrence counts and totals, a list of items depicted on the picture cards, a list of activities for production practice and carryover outside of intervention, and suggested extension activities. Appendix A summarizes the target patterns and language skills emphasized in each storybook. The CD-ROM contains black-and-white and color versions of the storybooks in two sizes, black-and-white and color versions of the sequence cards, and black-and-white picture cards—all in Portable Document Format (PDF) for printing.

Session Overview

Phonological sessions begin with a short period of auditory bombardment targeting the sound pattern for that session. Children listen carefully while the clinician reads or says aloud a list of 10–15 single words (from the word count list[s] for the story) that contain the target pattern. Slight amplification using binaural amplifiers is recommended. Small amplifiers, headsets, and connectors are available for a nominal cost at electronic supply stores (e.g., RadioShack). Visual and tactile cues should be used to emphasize the target pattern.

Next, children create their own picture cards for stimulable target words (usually three to five pictures per session). The story's picture cards can be photocopied from the corresponding unit or printed from the CD-ROM ahead of time for children to color, or children can draw their own pictures to color. Target words can be elicited during this step by requiring children to ask for the picture cards they want to color next or by having them tell what they have colored when they are finished. More intense production practice is then conducted by incorporating the picture cards and target words into structured play or learning activities (usually two or three per session). Sessions conclude with another short period of auditory bombardment. Stimulability probing for the next session's target words can be conducted at the end of the session as well. The following sections describe how to use the materials within a session.

Storybooks

Use one or more of these activities to incorporate the storybook into a phonological remediation session:

- Photocopy the black-and-white story pages from the chosen unit, or print the black-and-white storybooks from the *More Make-n-Takes Software Companion.* Or, using a color inkjet or color laser printer connected to your computer or network, print the color storybooks from the accompanying CD-ROM. All stories may be printed as either full-size (11" wide by 8½" high) or child-size (5½" wide by 4¼" high). Directions for assembling the storybooks may be found in Appendix B or in the Table of Contents file on the CD-ROM. Use the storybooks for clinician-directed activities.

- Read the storybook aloud to children to model the target sound and to provide meaningful contexts to use the practice words.

- As children become familiar with the story line and the pictures, let them finish lines with target words or repeat words that you say.

- While reading, ask questions that require children to use target words to answer.

- For younger children or children with shorter attention spans, break the stories into shorter segments to read during each session or have the children act out the stories as they are read.

- Target question comprehension skills by asking questions about the story as you read it or by asking questions at the end of the story.

- Model and encourage predicting and problem solving as stories unfold.

- Reinforce number concepts by counting objects in the illustrations and pointing out examples of one-to-one correspondence.

- Print and assemble the child-size black-and-white storybook from the *More Make-n-Takes Software Companion,* following the instructions in Appendix B. Make a personal book for each child.

- Have children color the target words on the pages of their personal child-size storybook.

- Send the personal child-size storybooks home with suggestions for home activities.

Refer to the Production Practice and Carryover Activities in each unit for additional ideas.

Sequence Cards

Use these language development activities to improve comprehension, sequencing, story structure, and memory skills:

- Tell the story using the sequence cards. Encourage children to help tell the story using target words.

- Have children recall events and sequence the pictures according to the story.

- Give simple directions to have children create new sequences with the pictures.

- Adjust the number of pictures to use in the sequence according to the child's ability and age.

- Allow children to create their own sequences and explain them to you using the same terms.

- Model and prompt use of the terms *first, second, next,* and *last* to tell the sequence.

- Use the sequence cards for visual memory tasks. Present a series of cards, then have children close their eyes while you remove one of the pictures. Have children tell which picture is missing.

- Target question comprehension skills and number concepts using single cards.

Picture Cards

Use these activities to individualize sessions:

- Determine stimulability by having children imitate potential target words you model. Use visual and tactile cues to help elicit target sounds. Avoid words with phonetic environments that may interfere with correct production of the target sound because of assimilation. For example, if a child is substituting /t/ for /k/, the use of target words that also contain /t/ (e.g., *cat* or *kit*) is likely to hinder correct production of the /k/ sound because of assimilation.

- Once each child's stimulable words are identified, photocopy the appropriate pictures to make individual picture cards.

- Children can help cut, color, and glue the pictures onto index cards and then use them for a variety of activities designed to elicit correct productions. The majority of the pictures are directly related to the story; however, there are some unrelated words that can be used for production practice and incorporated into activities that tie into the story.

- Use picture cards for new activities. For example, use a child's individual practice cards from *To the Top of Mount Tip Tap* as sights to see on a hike around the room.

Word Count Lists

Use the Word Count Lists for these remediation and home activities:

- Use the corresponding word list(s) for each story to make individualized auditory bombardment lists for remediation sessions. Select 10–15 words from the list(s) and read them aloud at the beginning and end of each session. It is generally better to select words that are not being used for production practice, since children are asked to only listen to these words. (Oftentimes when a child hears a word that he or she has been asked to practice saying, it is difficult for the child to refrain from saying it during the listening time. The listening task is confused with the production task.) Ideally, children listen with headsets to receive amplification while the speech-language pathologist speaks into a microphone. If amplification is not available, the words are still read aloud.

- Send a copy of the word count list home when beginning a new target. Encourage caregivers to read the list aloud to their child daily (ideally two times per day) to facilitate awareness of the target pattern and to promote carryover to different settings. Remind caregivers that their child is only to listen to the words on the word list, not try to repeat them.

Picture Card Lists

Use the picture card list(s) as a reference for the picture cards available in each unit. The list(s) may also be used to generate a word list for auditory bombardment.

Production Practice and Carryover Activities

Use these suggestions to enhance the effectiveness of phonological remediation:

- Select activities from this list of ideas to elicit target sounds or patterns for each story. Activities are related to the theme or target words of the stories. They include use of both real objects and picture cards.

- Use these activities for production practice during remediation sessions.

- Send activities home for carryover practice.

Extension Activities

Use these suggested activities for all children who will benefit from language remediation or enrichment in a variety of settings:

- Use these ideas to facilitate a variety of language and literacy skills, including rhyming, vocabulary, semantics, syntax and morphology, sequencing, and critical thinking.

- Speech-language pathologists can monitor and reinforce sound production skills during breaks in phonological cycles while using the materials to address a variety of language skills.

- Classroom teachers can use the storybooks and sequence cards in the classroom setting to address concepts that all children need to develop (e.g., rhyming, sequencing, or storytelling) and at the same time provide a natural setting for identified children to transfer their phonological skills.

- Use Appendix A to find skills addressed by extension activities for each story.

The Role of Caregivers

Involvement from caregivers plays an important role in the success of any child's learning. Ongoing consultation and communication with caregivers is vital for them to understand the goals of the program and the techniques they can use at home to facilitate carryover of learning to natural settings. *More Make-n-Takes* includes a variety of practice and extension activities that can be shared with caregivers.

- During phonological intervention, send home corresponding auditory bombardment lists to be read daily. These lists contain a variety of words that use the target pattern. Remind parents that the child should only listen to the words and repeat them.

- Select picture cards that the child produces correctly and send them home after each session, along with suggestions for how to use the cards in play activities. Explain to caregivers the visual and tactile cues they can use to help elicit the target sound from their child.

More

Measuring Progress

Measure phonological progress formally by readministering an assessment tool such as *The Assessment of Phonological Processes–Revised* (Hodson, 1986) at the end of a cycle. During sessions, make anecdotal notes describing individual children's productions, the types of cues they require, and environments where they are successful with productions (e.g., small-group setting, classroom, or home) to keep track of progress and carryover that may be occurring. For traditional articulation intervention, chart and collect data of correct and incorrect productions.

Appendices

Summary of Target Patterns and Extension Activity Skills

		Big Baseball Game Today!	Our Big, Lazy Pig	Five Fun Clowns	To the Top of Mount Tip Tap	Rat-a-Tat-Tat and a Toot and a Tweet	Mack and the Yak Horn Stew	Our Magic Car in the Country	Two Ghosts and a Goblin
Target Patterns	**Syllableness** Two syllables	●							
	Three syllables	●							
	Initial Consonants /p/		●						
	/m/		●						
	/w/		●						
	Final Consonants /m/			●					
	/n/			●					
	/p/				●				
	/t/					●			
	Final Velars /k/						●		
	Initial Velars and Initial Glottals /k/							●	
	/g/								●
	/h/								●
Extension Activity Skills	Rhyming	●	●	●	●	●	●	●	●
	Vocabulary Development	●	●	●	●	●	●	●	●
	Synonyms								●
	Antonyms	●							
	Attributes						●		
	Associations		●						
	Basic Concepts			●					
	Multiple-Meaning Words						●		
	Absurdities					●		●	
	Classification					●			●
	Analogies	●							
	Plurals	●							
	Possessives						●		
	Third-Person Singular Verbs			●		●			
	Present Progressive Verbs							●	
	Past Tense Verbs				●				●
	Question Comprehension		●						
	Sequencing						●		
	Critical Thinking	●	●	●	●	●	●	●	●

How to Create a Full-Size Black-and-White Storybook

What You'll Need

- Adobe Acrobat Reader® 5.0 or higher (If you don't already have Acrobat Reader installed on your computer, you must first install the program to your hard drive. You can download a free copy from http://www.adobe.com.

- A photocopier, or an inkjet or laser printer connected to your computer or computer network (To avoid ink bleedthrough, you may want to use heavy-stock paper.)

- A comb- or spiral-binding system or other fasteners (If you'd rather not bind the book yourself, print shops, photocopy shops, and office-supply stores [e.g., Office Max or Staples] offer affordable binding services. Check your local listings for availability.)

If you photocopy the pages from the book:

1. Tear out the storybook pages along the perforation. (If you choose not to remove the pages, the perforation helps the pages lie flat on the copy machine). Photocopy the pages from the book in a two-sided, landscape format. (Your page width should be 11" and page height 8½".)

2. (Before you bind the book together, it is recommended that you include a sheet of clear acetate over the front and back cover of the book or laminate them for durability and protection.) Collect the pages into the proper page sequence and secure with a fastener, such as a comb, spiral, or plastic binding, or metal or plastic rings. Trim the excess binding away, if necessary (see diagram on next page).

If you print the story from the CD-ROM:

1. Under File > Page Setup, select "Landscape" page orientation. (Your page width should be 11" and page height 8½".) Under File > Print, navigate to and select "Odd Pages Only." Print all odd-numbered pages, flip your printed stack over, and insert the printed pages in your printer's paper tray. Under File > Print, navigate to and select "Even Pages Only." Double-check your page orientation and page order to ensure that you print the book properly as two-sided. (Alternatively, you may print all pages single-sided from

your printer and use a duplexing photocopier to make the pages double-sided.)

2. (Before you bind the book together, it is recommended that you include a sheet of clear acetate over the front and back cover of the book or laminate them for durability and protection.) Collect the pages into the proper page sequence and secure with a fastener, such as a comb, spiral, or plastic binding, or metal or plastic rings. Trim the excess binding away, if necessary (see diagram below).

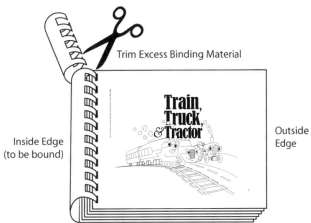

Binding your book as described in Step 2 allows for the largest possible viewing format, suitable for reading to a class or small group. When you're finished, a typical page spread in each book should resemble the diagram below.

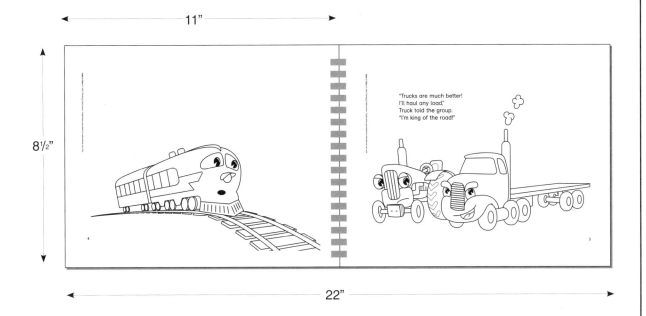

How to Create a Child-Size Black-and-White Storybook

What You'll Need

- Adobe Acrobat Reader® 5.0 or higher (If you don't already have Acrobat Reader installed on your computer, you must first install the program to your hard drive. You can download a free copy from http://www.adobe.com.)

- A photocopier, or an inkjet or laser printer connected to your computer or computer network (To avoid ink bleedthrough, you may wish to use heavy-stock paper.)

- A stapler or other fasteners and glue or tape

---

1. Under File > Page Setup, select "Landscape" page orientation. (Your page width should be 11" and page height 8½".) Under File > Print, navigate to and select "Odd Pages Only." Print all odd-numbered pages, flip your printed stack over, and insert the printed pages in your printer's paper tray. Under File > Print, navigate to and select "Even Pages Only." Double-check your page orientation and page order to ensure that you print the book properly as two-sided. (Alternatively, you may print all pages single-sided from your printer and use a duplexing photocopier to make the pages double-sided.)

2. Trim then fold each page pair along the appropriate guidelines (see diagram below).

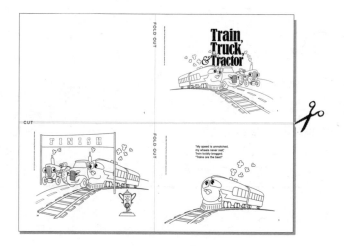

3. Collect the pages into the proper page sequence and secure along the left side with a stapler or other fastener, such as a comb, spiral, or plastic binding, or metal or plastic rings. Trim the excess binding away, if necessary (see diagram below). Depending on the length of the story, the center pages may be blank. Use glue or transparent tape along the edge of these pages to secure them together.

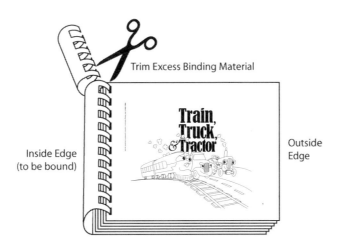

When you're finished, a typical page spread in each book should resemble the diagram below.

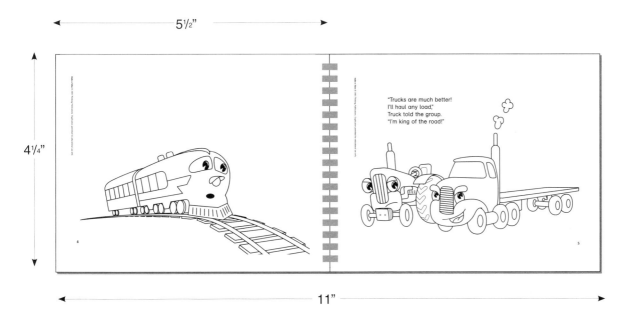

How to Create a Full-Size Color Storybook

What You'll Need

- Adobe Acrobat Reader® 5.0 or higher (If you don't already have Acrobat Reader installed on your computer, you must first install the program to your hard drive. You can download a free copy from http://www.adobe.com.

- A color inkjet or color laser printer connected to your computer or computer network (To avoid ink bleedthrough, you may wish to use heavy-stock paper.)

- Glue or double-stick tape

- A comb- or spiral-binding system or other fasteners (If you'd rather not bind the book yourself, print shops, photocopy shops, and office-supply stores [e.g., Office Max or Staples] offer affordable binding services. Check your local listings for availability.)

---

1. Under File > Page Setup, select "Landscape" page orientation. (Your page width should be 11" and page height 8½".) Under File > Print, navigate to and select "Odd Pages Only." Print all odd-numbered pages, flip your printed stack over, and insert the printed pages in your color printer's paper tray. Under File > Print, navigate to and select "Even Pages Only." Double-check your page orientation and page order to ensure that you print the book properly as two-sided. (Alternatively, you may print all pages single-sided from your color printer and then use glue or double-sided tape to seal the blank sides of the pages together.)

2. (Before you bind the book together, it is recommended that you include a sheet of clear acetate over the front and back cover of the book or laminate them for durability and protection.) Collect the pages into the proper page sequence and secure with a fastener, such as a comb, spiral, or plastic binding, or metal or plastic rings. Trim the excess binding away, if necessary (see diagram that follows).

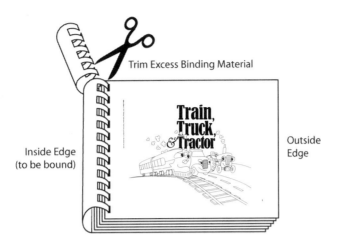

Inside Edge
(to be bound)

Trim Excess Binding Material

Outside
Edge

Binding your book as described in Step 2 allows for the largest possible viewing format, suitable for reading to a class or small group. When you're finished, a typical page spread in each book should resemble the diagram below.

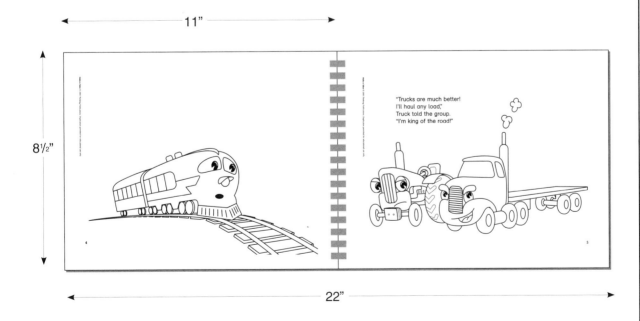

How to Create a Child-Size Color Storybook

What You'll Need

- Adobe Acrobat Reader® 5.0 or higher (If you don't already have Acrobat Reader installed on your computer, you must first install the program to your hard drive. You can download a free copy from http://www.adobe.com.

- A color inkjet or color laser printer connected to your computer or computer network (To avoid ink bleedthrough, you may wish to use heavy-stock paper.)

- A stapler or other fasteners and glue or tape

---

1. Under File > Page Setup, select "Landscape" page orientation. (Your page width should be 11" and page height 8½".) Under File > Print, navigate to and select "Odd Pages Only." Print all odd-numbered pages, flip your printed stack over, and insert the printed pages in your color printer's paper tray. Under File > Print, navigate to and select "Even Pages Only." Double-check your page orientation and page order to ensure that you print the book properly as two-sided.

2. Trim and fold each page pair along the appropriate guidelines (see diagram below).

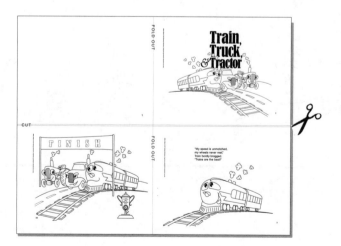

3. Collect the pages into the proper page sequence and secure along the left side with a stapler or other fastener, such as a comb, spiral, or plastic binding, or metal or plastic rings. Trim the excess binding away, if necessary (see diagram below). Depending on the length of the story, the center pages may be blank. Use glue or transparent tape along the edge of these pages to secure them together.

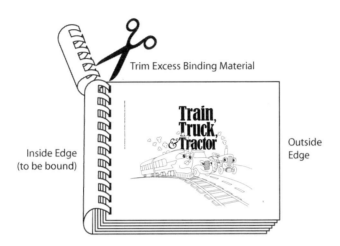

Trim Excess Binding Material

Inside Edge
(to be bound)

Outside Edge

When you're finished, a typical page spread in each book should resemble the diagram below.

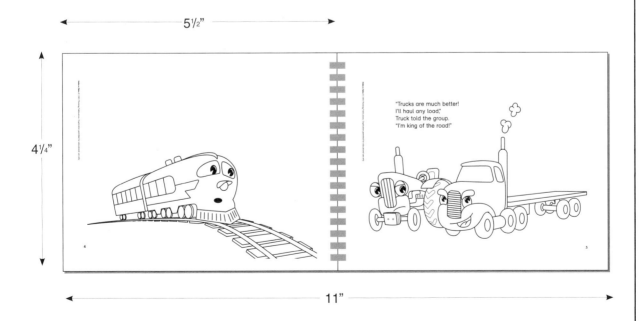

More

References

Burns, M.S., Griffin, P., and Snow, C. (Eds.). (1999). *Starting out right: A guide to promoting children's reading success.* Washington, DC: National Academy Press.

Gansen, C., and Gansen, E. (2003). *More make-n-takes.* Greenville, SC: Super Duper Publications.

Hodson, B. (1986). *The Assessment of Phonological Processes–Revised.* Austin, TX: Pro-Ed.

Hodson, B.W. (1997). Disordered phonologies: What have we learned about assessment and treatment? In B. Hodson and M. Edwards (Eds.), *Perspectives in applied phonology* (pp. 197–224). New York: Aspen.

Hodson, B.W. (2000, March). Enhancing phonological and metaphonological skills: What we know in the year 2000. Presentation at the annual convention of the Wisconsin Speech-Language-Hearing Association, Milwaukee, WI.

Hodson, B.W., and Paden, E.P. (1991). *Targeting intelligible speech: A phonological approach to remediation* (2nd ed.). Austin, TX: Pro-Ed.

Hodson, B.W., Scherz, J.A., and Strattman, K.H. (2002). Evaluating communicative abilities of a highly unintelligible preschooler. *American Journal of Speech-Language Pathology, 11,* 236–242.

The 8 Great Storybook Units

Big Baseball Game Today!

Hooray! Hooray!
We see a game today!
Bye-bye, Mama.
Hurry up, Papa!
Let's get on our way.

Ticket taker,
take our ticket.
We're inside the park.
Hurry, Papa, find our seats.
Soon the game will start.

Baseball cap, baseball bat,
uniform, and glove.
Green grass, ice-cream cone,
sunshine up above.

Popcorn, peanuts,
pop, and bubble gum.
Hamburger, Popsicle,
hot dog in a bun.

Hooray! Hooray!
Big baseball game today!
Infield, outfield,
the baseball players play.

Pitcher, catcher, first base,
second base, and third.
Pop up, fly out,
grounder in the dirt.

"Come on, batter, swing your bat!"
Hear the people scream.
Ball two! Strike one!
Hit one for our team!

8

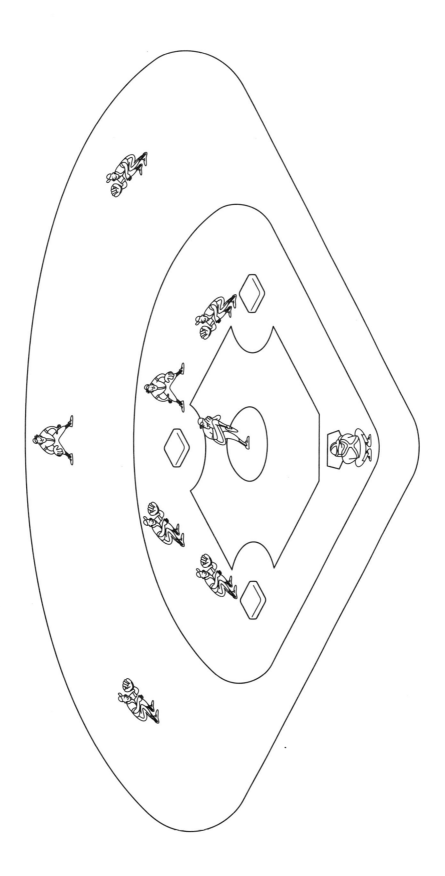

Hooray! Hooray!
Big baseball game today!
Our team just hit the ball
a long, long way!

Run to first.
Run to second.
Slide into third base.
Hooray! Hooray!
The umpire calls him safe.

Batter up! Throw the pitch!
The score is tied at one.
CRACK, BOOM, the baseball flies—
Jeepers! A home run!

Ho! Ho! What a game!
The crowd roars at the play!
Hooray! Hooray!
Our team has won the day!

Night-night, we're back at home,
asleep and all tucked in.
Dreaming all night long
of what a fun day it's been.

Baseball cap, baseball bat,
uniform, and glove.
Green grass, ice-cream cone,
sunshine up above.

Popcorn, peanuts,
pop, and bubble gum.
Hamburger, Popsicle,
hot dog in a bun.

Pitcher, catcher, first base,
second base, and third.
Pop up, fly out,
grounder in the dirt.

Infield, outfield,
the baseball players play.
Hooray! Hooray!
Our team played great today!

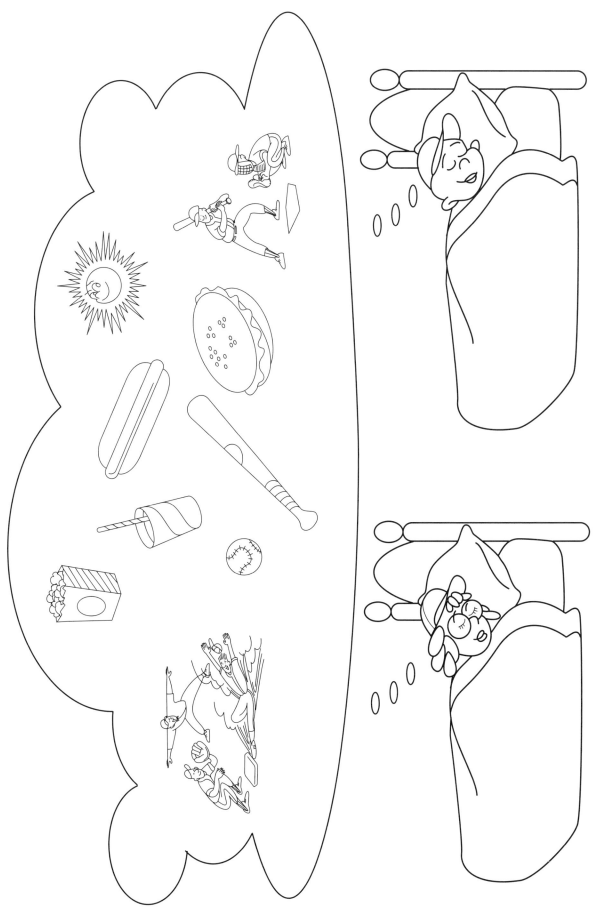

Sequence Cards

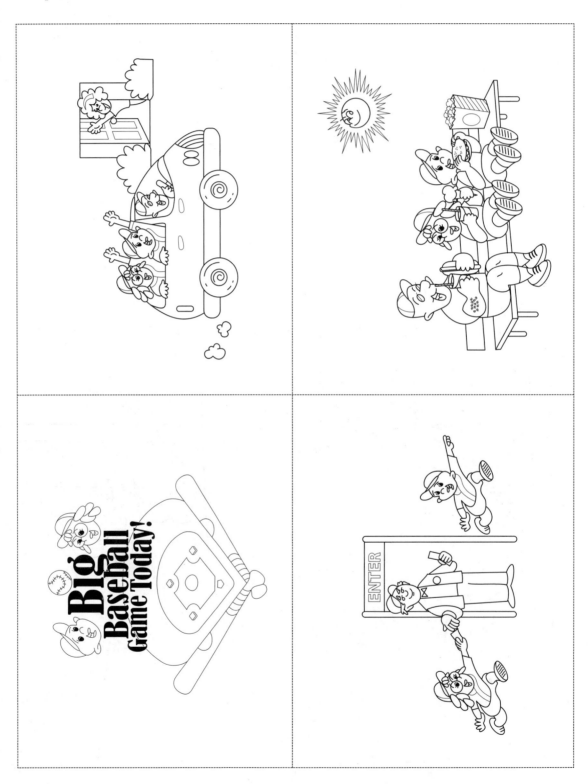

Sequence Cards

Sequence Cards

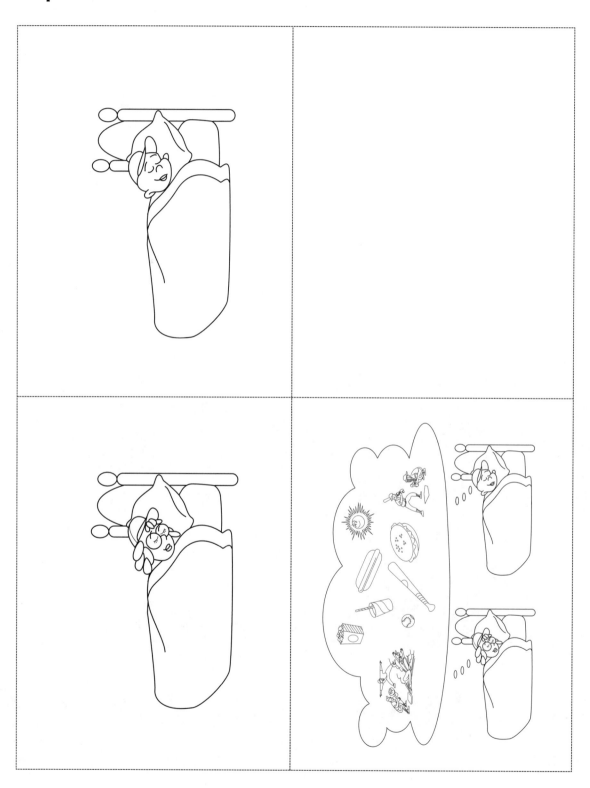

Picture Cards

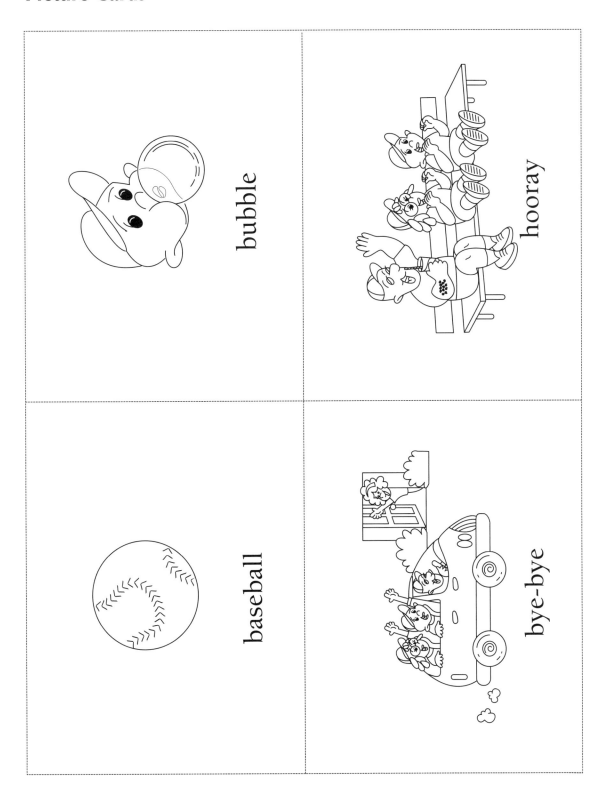

bubble

hooray

baseball

bye-bye

Picture Cards

Mama

peanuts

hot dog

Papa

Picture Cards

rainbow

ticket

popcorn

sunshine

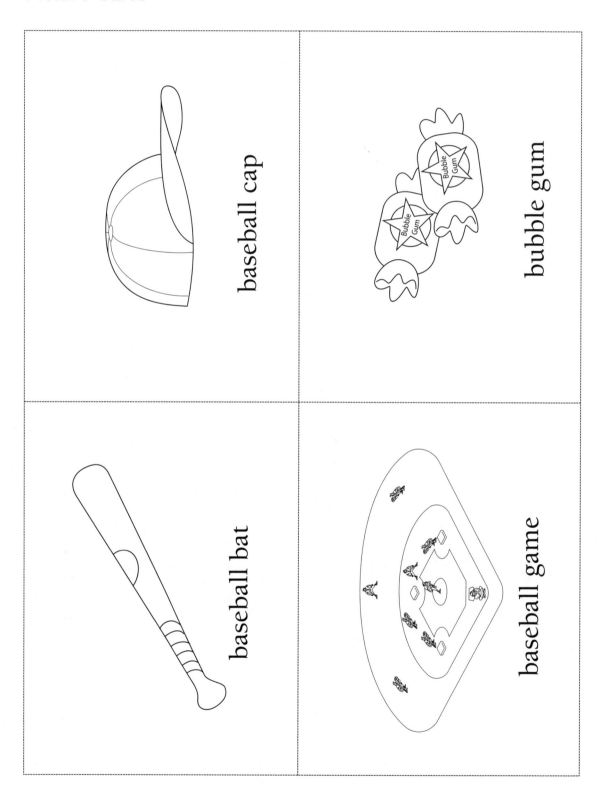

baseball cap

bubble gum

baseball bat

baseball game

Picture Cards

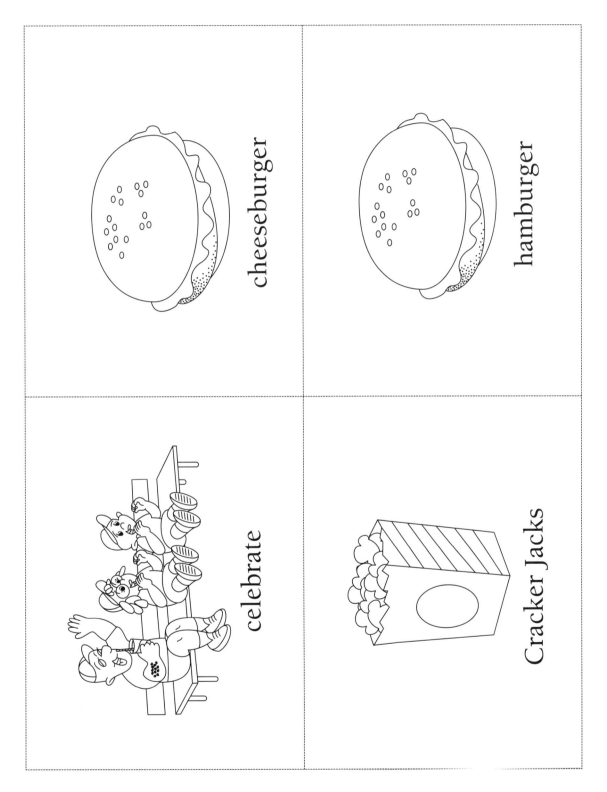

cheeseburger

hamburger

celebrate

Cracker Jacks

Picture Cards

ice-cream cone

uniform

hot dog bun

Popsicle

Word Count Lists

Two Syllables				**Three Syllables**	
Word	Frequency	Word	Frequency	Word	Frequency
above	2	Mama	1	baseball bat	2
asleep	1	night-night	1	baseball cap	2
baseball	3	outfield	2	baseball game	2
batter	2	Papa	2	bubble gum	2
bye-bye	1	peanuts	2	hamburger	2
catcher	2	people	1	ice-cream cone	2
dreaming	1	pitcher	2	Popsicle	2
first base	2	players	2	second base	2
grounder	2	popcorn	2	uniform	2
home run	1	second	1		
hooray	12	sunshine	2		
hot dog	2	taker	1		
hurry	2	third base	1		
infield	2	ticket	2		
inside	1	today	4		
into	1	umpire	1		
jeepers	1				
		Total Words: 65		**Total Words: 18**	

Picture Card Lists

Two Syllables	**Three Syllables**
baseball	baseball bat
bubble	baseball cap
bye-bye	baseball game
hooray	bubble gum
hot dog	celebrate
Mama	cheeseburger
Papa	Cracker Jacks
peanuts	hamburger
popcorn	hot dog bun
rainbow	ice-cream cone
sunshine	Popsicle
ticket	uniform

Production Practice and Carryover Activities

- Play **baseball**: The **pitcher** hands the **batter** a target picture card. The **batter** names the card and then spins a **spinner** or rolls a die to see how many **bases** to run.

- Make **popcorn** and eat it for a snack.

- Blow **bubbles**.

- Chew **bubble gum**.

- Cheer **hooray** while playing a game.

- Make and eat **ice-cream cones** or **sundaes**. Let children say which they want.

- Use **play dough** to make various foods (e.g., **hot dogs**, **hamburgers**, **cheeseburgers**, **French fries**, or **cupcakes**).

- **Finger-paint** a picture.

- Cut **tickets** out of **paper**. Use them to go to a pretend **baseball game**.

- Play **jump rope**.

Extension Activities

Rhyming

- Do these words rhyme? (yes or no)

hurry - hot dog	bubble - double
today - hooray	Papa - pitcher
ticket - wicket	home run - hamburger
Mama - llama	baseball hat - baseball bat
sunshine - rainbow	jeepers - creepers

- Which words rhyme?

ticket - thicket - pitcher	pajamas - llamas - bedtime
batter - hurry - scurry	hula hoop - baseball - ice-cream scoop
trouble - first base - double	dreaming - scheming - sleeping
popcorn - foghorn - nachos	celebrate - infield fly - paper plate
popcorn - yummy - tummy	June - September - December

- Tell a word that rhymes with *today, worry, puppy, patter, sleeping, mother, keepers, grounder, hurry, cricket.* (Thinking of two- or three-syllable rhyming words may be very difficult. Consider accepting nonsense words for this task. Another option would be to have children count the number of syllables in words that you say aloud to them.)

Vocabulary Development

- Read the story and discuss vocabulary that may be new to students: *uniform, infield, outfield, pitcher, catcher, pop up, grounder, batter, ball, strike, umpire, safe, tied, home run, batter up.*

Antonyms

- Use the story context to introduce the idea of opposites. Demonstrate the opposites *throw-catch* and *pitcher-catcher* using a ball. Point out other opposites within the context of a baseball game: *win-lose, infield-outfield, safe-out, hit-miss (strike).*

Analogies

- Use the vocabulary in the story to expose children to analogies involving opposites, characteristics, and functions. *Day is to night as win is to lose. Hot dog is to eat as pop is to drink. Bat is to swing as ball is to throw. Sun is to hot as Popsicle is to cold.*

Plurals

- Use the sequence cards or pairs of the black-and-white picture cards to elicit plural forms.

Critical Thinking

- Discuss winning and losing. *How do people feel when they win? When they lose? What are appropriate ways to act when we win and lose?* Role-play situations and have children demonstrate what is discussed.

Our Big Lazy Pig

and other animal rhymes

Our Big, Lazy Pig

What meal will make
our pig perk up
and leave his pile of muck?
Pudding pie? Mashed potatoes?
A Popsicle to suck?

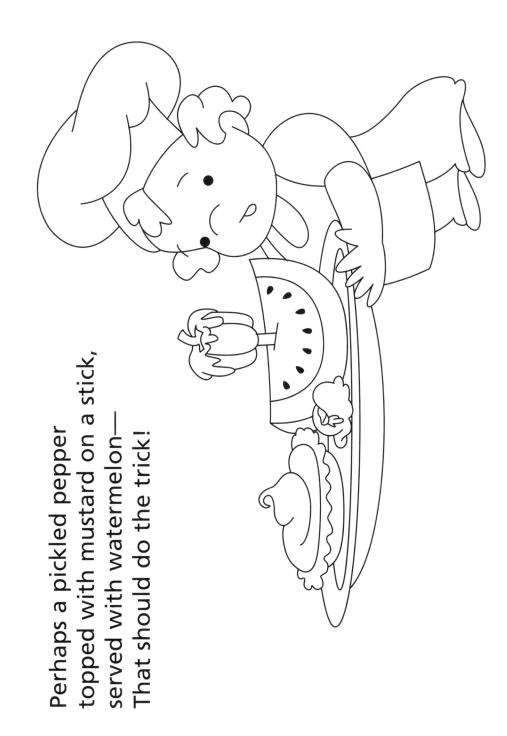

Perhaps a pickled pepper
topped with mustard on a stick,
served with watermelon—
That should do the trick!

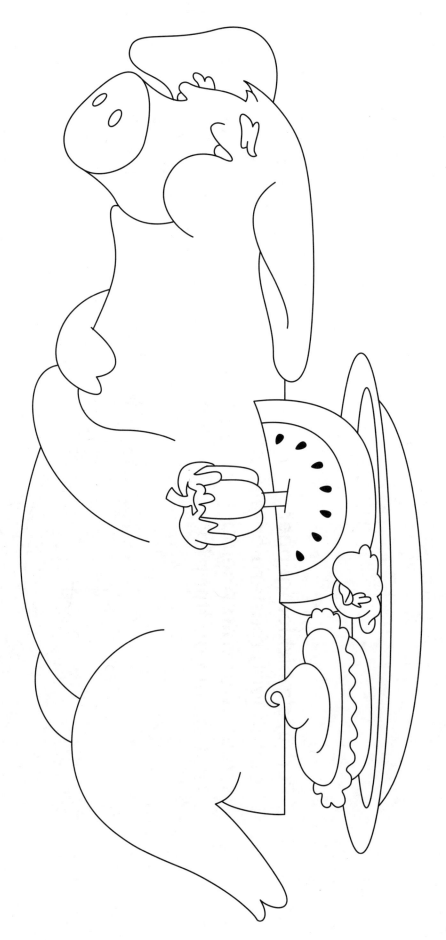

4

Or,
maybe warmed-up waffles
topped with melted cheese.
Peas and peaches on the side
and lots of meatballs, please.

Our big, fat, lazy pig won't budge.
That pig just won't get out.
Too lazy muddling in the mud
to move his lazy snout.

Since our big, lazy pig won't move,
that means our story's done.
Maybe you could make a meal
that gets that pig to run!

Mrs. Milk Cow

Where is Mrs. Milk Cow?
In the meadow, munching grass.
We sit and watch quietly
and wait for her to pass.

It's peaceful in the meadow,
beneath the sky so blue.
Watch for Mrs. Milk Cow.
Listen for her "Moo."

Old Miss Spider

Where does old Miss Spider
weave her web at dawn?
In the pink petunia patch
and pansies in the lawn.

In the morning mist it sparkles.
She weaves it perfectly.
What a masterpiece she's made—
so wonderful to see.

Mr. Mouse

Why does Mr. Mouse insist
on wearing mini-mittens?
They're nice and warm and made of wool
so paws won't be frostbitten.

It's chilly in his pumpkin patch
when winter winds whip through.
He runs inside to warm himself
with a bowl of pumpkin stew.

Monkey Mess

What do all the monkeys do
on Mondays for their fun?
Play pinball in pajamas
and Ping-Pong in the sun.

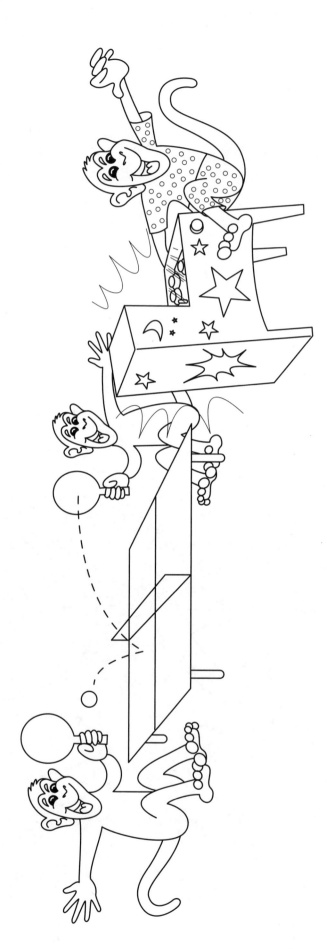

At night they order pizza,
a pepperoni pie.
Whoops! They spill a mug of pop.
A monkey mess. Oh my!

Papa Puddle

When will Papa Puddle take
his family for a swim?
At one o'clock each afternoon,
they all jump in with him.

They follow Papa in and out
and through the tall pond weeds.
They waddle back to Mother's nest,
made of moss and reeds.

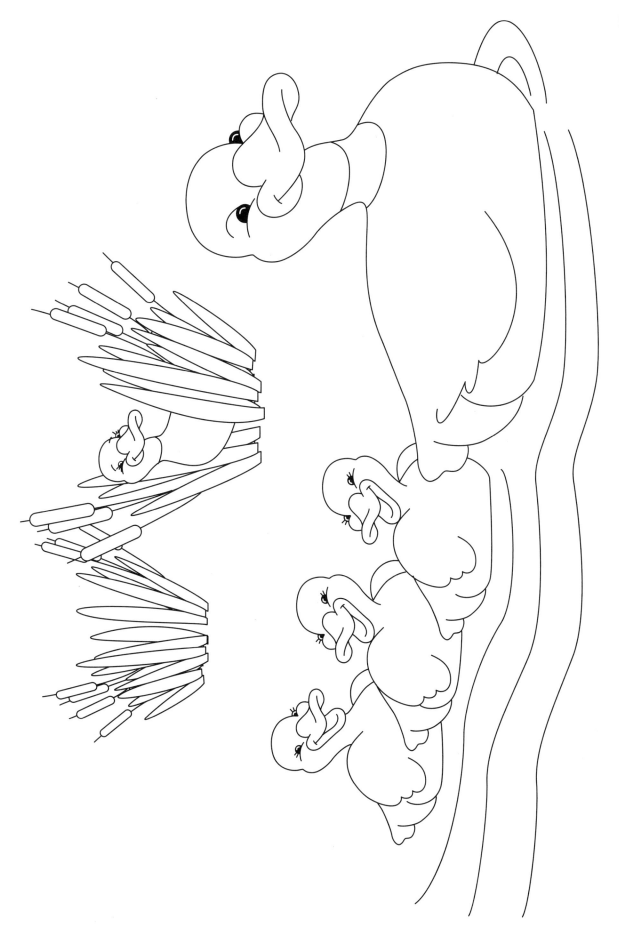

Wee Winnie Wiener Dog

Which Wiener dog will wag her tail
faster than the rest?
Wee Winnie will—make no mistake!
She wants to be the best.

Wee Winnie minds her manners
and makes her master proud.
She picks the paper up at night
and never barks too loud.

Wally Walrus

What could be this silly game
Wally Walrus plays up north?
He bounces a ball with polka dots
and rolls it back and forth.

In winter snow so white and deep,
he'll pop it in his mouth.
It's not unlike what penguins play
at the other pole down south.

Sequence Cards

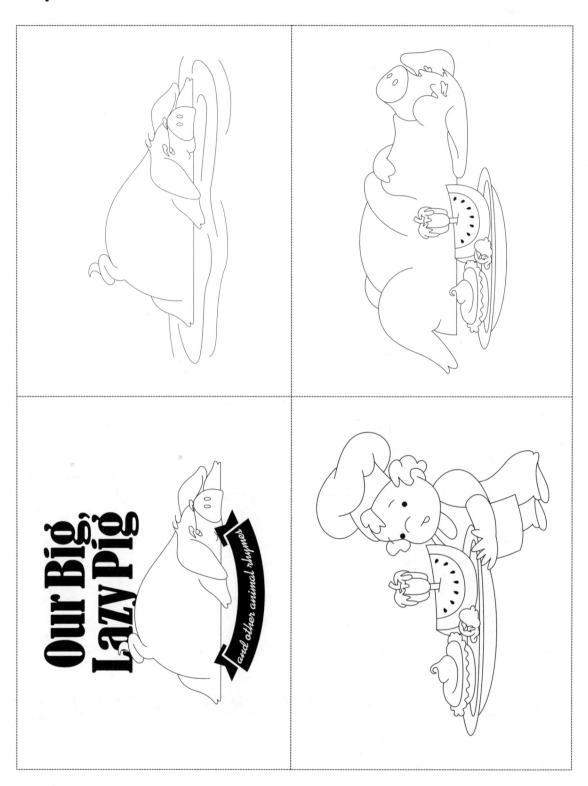

Sequence Cards

Old Miss Spider

Mrs. Milk Cow

Sequence Cards

Sequence Cards

Picture Cards

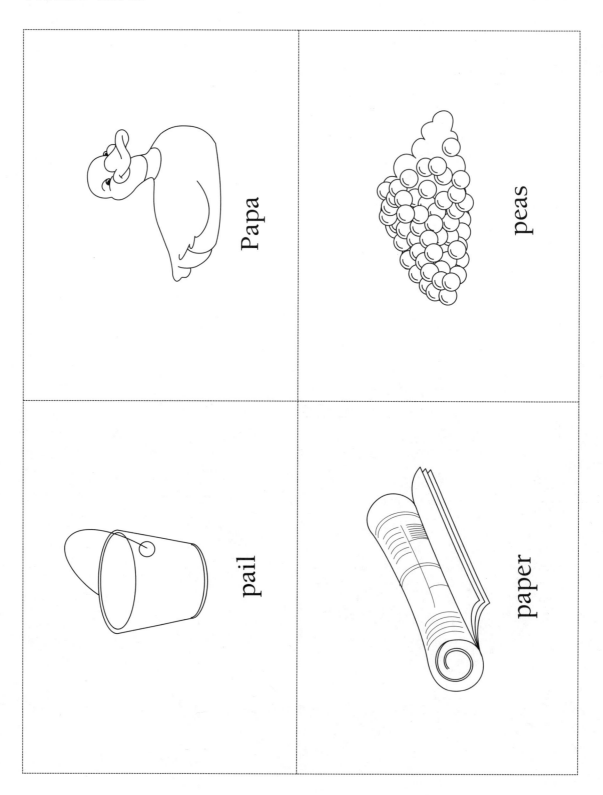

Picture Cards

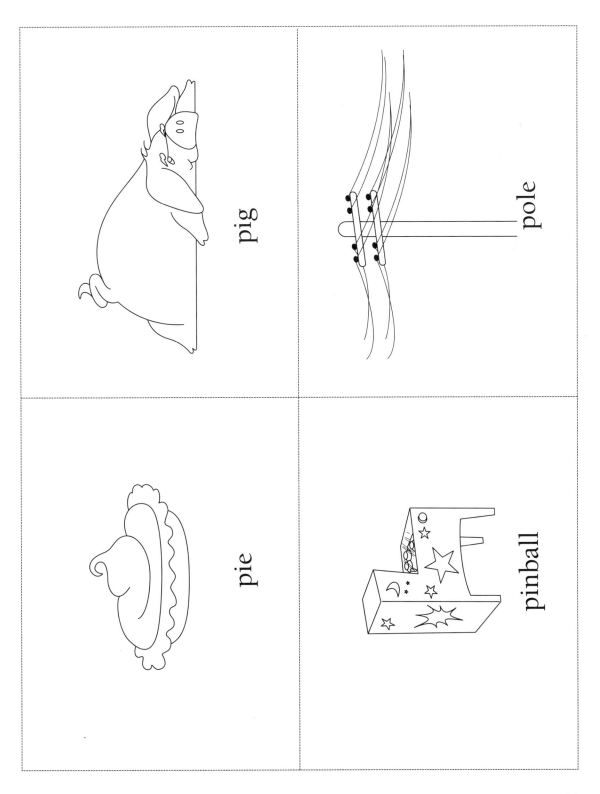

pig

pole

pie

pinball

Picture Cards

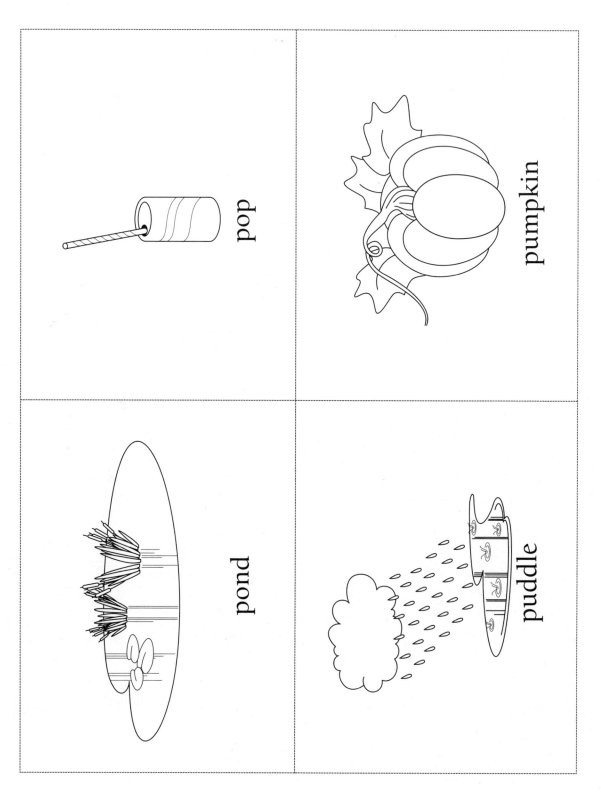

pop

pumpkin

pond

puddle

Picture Cards

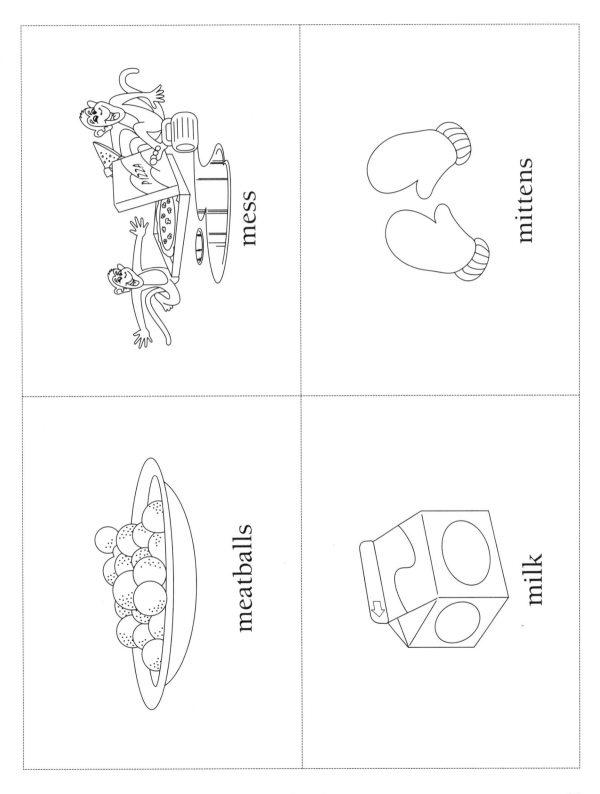

mess

mittens

meatballs

milk

Picture Cards

moo

mouse

monkey

mother

Picture Cards

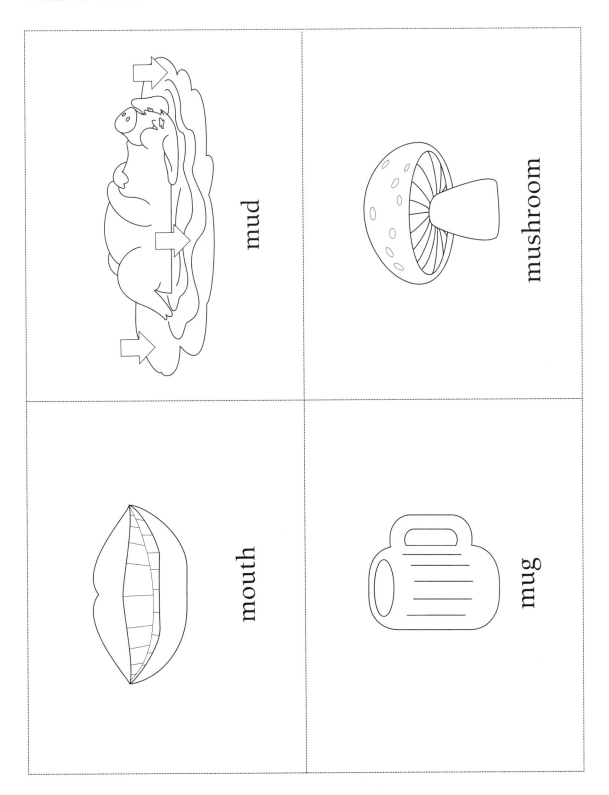

mud

mushroom

mouth

mug

Picture Cards

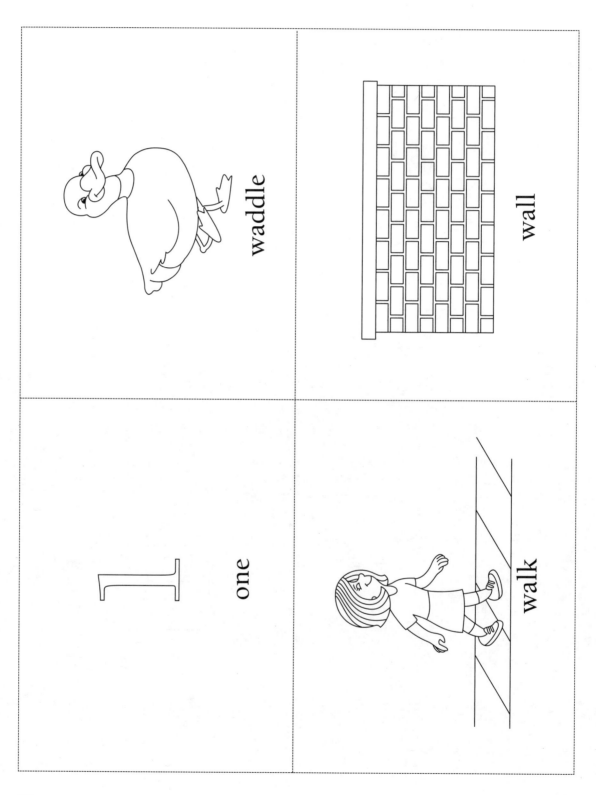

waddle

wall

one

walk

Picture Cards

Picture Cards

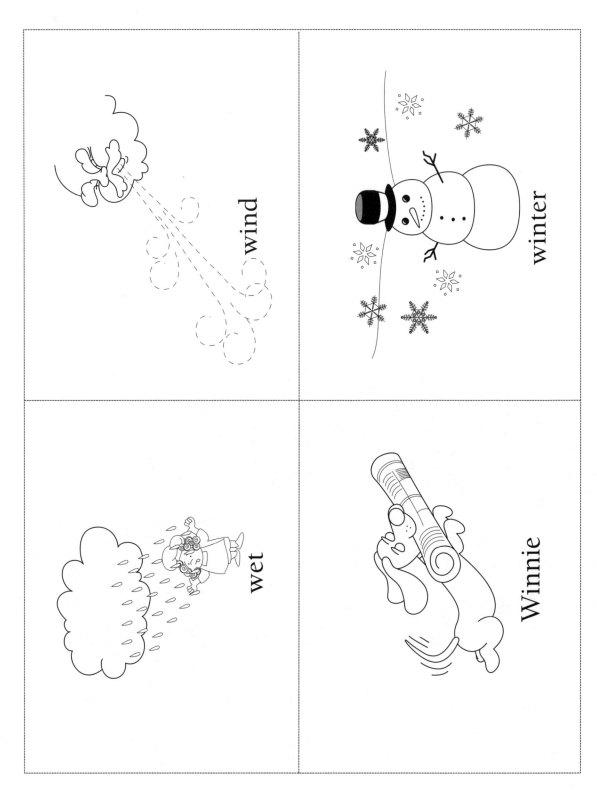

wind

winter

wet

Winnie

Word Count Lists

Initial /p/		Initial /m/		Initial /w/	
Word	Frequency	Word	Frequency	Word	Frequency
pajamas	1	made	3	one	1
pansies	1	make	3	waddle	1
Papa	2	makes	1	waffles	1
paper	1	manners	1	wag	1
pass	1	mashed	1	wait	1
patch	2	master	1	Wally	1
paws	1	masterpiece	1	Walrus	1
peaceful	1	maybe	2	wants	1
peaches	1	meadow	2	warm	2
peas	1	meal	2	warmed-up	1
penguins	1	means	1	watch	2
pepper	1	meatballs	1	watermelon	1
pepperoni	1	melted	1	wearing	1
perfectly	1	mess	1	weave	1
perhaps	1	Milk	2	weaves	1
perk	1	minds	1	web	1
petunia	1	mini	1	Wee	2
pickled	1	Miss	1	weeds	1
picks	1	mist	1	what	5
pie	2	mistake	1	when	2
pig	5	mittens	1	where	2
pile	1	Mondays	1	which	1
pinball	1	monkey	1	whip	1
Ping-Pong	1	monkeys	1	white	1
pink	1	moo	1	whoops	1
pizza	1	morning	1	why	1
pole	1	moss	1	wiener	1
polka dots	1	Mother's	1	will	4
pond	1	Mouse	1	winds	1
pop	2	mouth	1	Winnie	2
Popsicle	1	move	2	winter	2
potatoes	1	Mr.	1	with	6
pudding	1	Mrs.	2	won't	4
puddle	1	muck	1	wonderful	1
pumpkin	2	mud	1	wool	1
		muddling	1		
		mug	1		
		munching	1		
		mustard	1		
		my	1		
Total Words: 44		**Total Words: 50**		**Total Words: 57**	

Picture Card Lists

Initial /p/	Initial /m/	Initial /w/
pail	meatballs	one
Papa	mess	waddle
paper	milk	walk
peas	mittens	wall
pie	monkey	Wally
pig	moo	water
pinball	mother	web
pole	mouse	weeds
pond	mouth	wet
pop	mud	wind
puddle	mug	Winnie
pumpkin	mushroom	winter

Production Practice and Carryover Activities

- Place **picture** cards in a **path** to the **pond**. Children **waddle** behind **Papa Puddle** to the **pond** and name the **pictures** that they **pass**.

- Drink **mugs** of **milk**, **pop**, or **water**.

- Make a **monkey pizza** with **mushrooms**, **pepperoni**, and cheese. Talk about how the cheese **melts** when the **pizza** is cooked.

- Pile **mittens** in the **middle** of the floor. Take turns **matching mittens**.

- **Pick** objects or **pictures** out of a **pail**.

- Cut target **pictures** into circles and tape them on a ball to **make polka** dots. Roll the ball back and forth. Have children name the **picture** that is on top when they catch the ball.

- **Make** a **meal** for the lazy **pig** by gluing **pictures** of food on a **paper** plate.

- Have children pretend they are are **Wee Winnie** the **wiener** dog. Take turns giving commands for **Winnie** to follow (*Winnie, roll over. Winnie, lay down. Winnie, bury your bone*).

- Draw a large spider **web** on **paper** and tape it to the **wall**. Tape target **pictures** face down on the **web**. Take turns turning **pictures** over and telling **what** is in the **web**.

- Build a **wall** out of blocks. Blow on the **wall** like the **wind** and try to knock it down.

Extension Activities

Rhyming

- Do these words rhyme? (yes or no)

pail - pack	wore - more
milk - wet	mouth - peas
wear - mare	pumpkin - winter
muddle - puddle	when - pen
pat - mat	mark - park

- Which words rhyme?

wet - met - pin	wash - pass - mass
won - pump - pun	pan - win - man

wee - meet - Pete   more - paper - wore

peep - week - meek   paint - poke - woke

make - pick - wick   moo - woo - mouse

- Tell a word that rhymes with *pen, pack, pig, mark, mud, make, mad, weed, wall, wish.*

Vocabulary Development

- Read the story and discuss vocabulary that may be new to students: *meadow, munching, weave, masterpiece, mug, insist, frostbitten, moss, reeds, muck, budge, muddling, perk up, minds her manners.*

Associations

- Present pictures or real objects that are associated with the animals in the stories. Discuss which animal goes with each item (*pig-mud, cow-milk, monkey-banana, mouse-cheese, dog-bone, spider-web*).

Question Comprehension

- Discuss the poems individually. Have children respond to the question asked in each of the rhymes.

Critical Thinking

- Talk about what kinds of food people need to eat. Discuss the major food groups. Give children a paper plate to write or draw the foods they would include to plan a healthy meal.

One fun clown
whose name is Pam
can balance a cane
and a ten-pound ham.

As the circus crowd
claps for Pam,
a second clown
climbs up that ham.

Two fun clowns
named Pam and Sam
stack a cane, a ham,
and a clown on Pam.

As people cheer
those two clowns on,
up climbs a third,
whose name is John.

When three fun clowns
stack a clown on a clown
on a ham on a cane
with Pam at the bottom,
the crowd goes insane.

They scream even more
when a fourth clown climbs
to the top with a hen
and nine green limes.

Four fun clowns,
whose names are Tim
and John and Sam
and Pam under him,
make some tall team—
Then another joins in!

A fifth fun clown,
named Jenny Jean, climbs
to the top of the stack
of the nine green limes
and the hen over Tim
over John and Sam
and the clown at the bottom,
whose name is Pam.

The clown at the top,
named Jenny Jean, then
puts a yam and a lamb
on top of her chin.

Balancing both,
she sticks out her thumb
and shows off a plum
and a worm chewing gum.

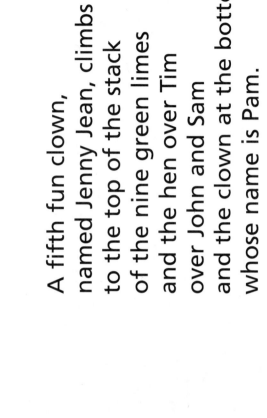

The crowd at the circus
goes wild at the sights
of five fun clowns
stacked clear to the lights.

The crowd goes quiet
and the lights go down.
A drum roll starts
and they watch each clown.

Jenny Jean stands
with the worm chewing gum
from a plum sticking out
on the end of her thumb.

The lamb and the yam
still sit on her chin
when an egg pops out
from the hen with Tim!

The egg drops down
from the hen with Tim
and bounces off John
still underneath him.

The egg flies by Sam
and goes to Pam,
balancing a cane with
a ten-pound ham.

Right at the time
that the egg should go SPLAT!
Pam has a pan
for the egg to splat flat!

Blam! Wham!
Fireworks pop!
It seems the cheers
will never stop.

Those five fun clowns
make quite a scene—
Pam, Sam, John, Tim,
and Jenny Jean.

A sight like this
has never been seen
before or since
or in between!

Sequence Cards

Sequence Cards

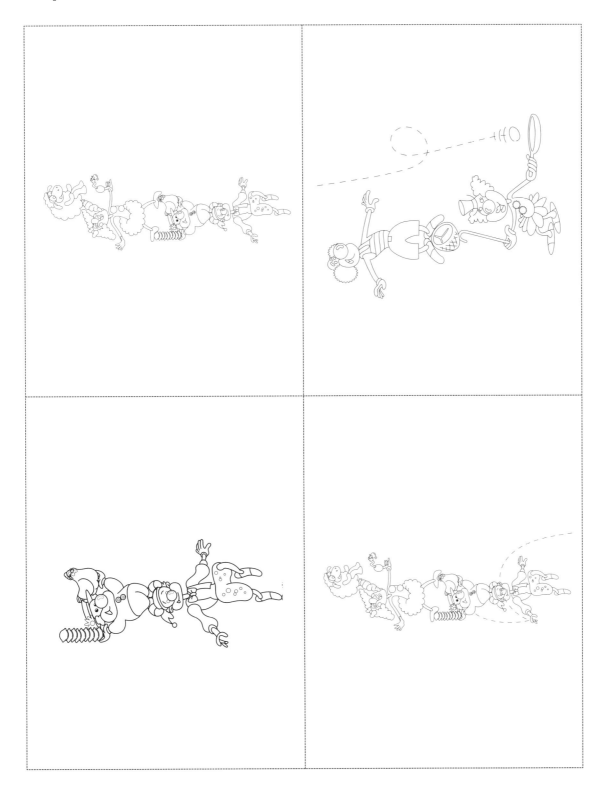

Sequence Cards

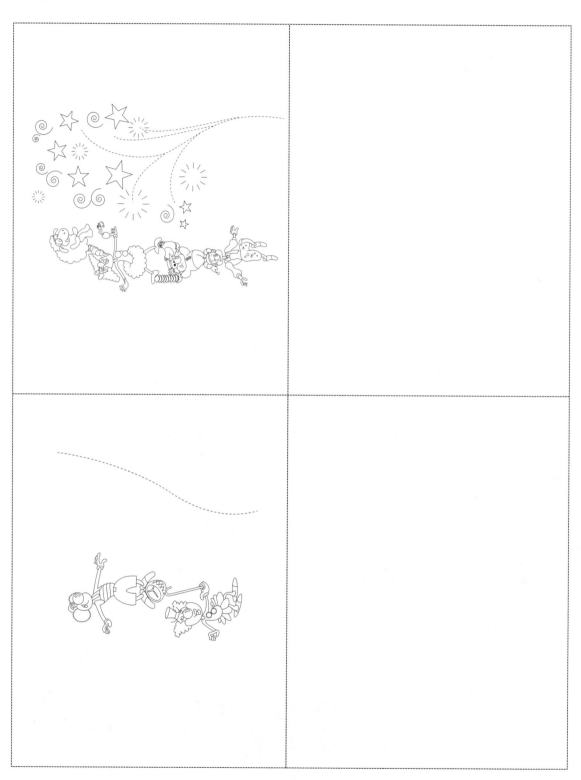

Picture Cards

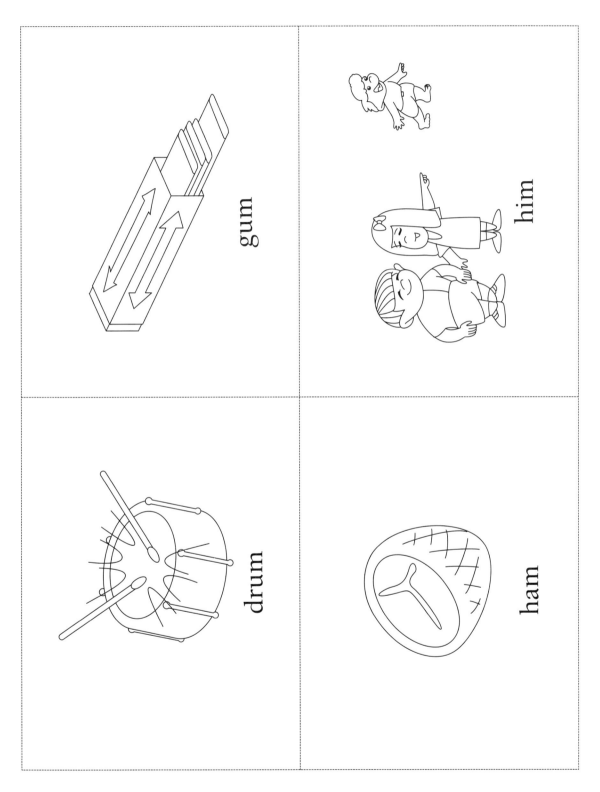

gum

him

drum

ham

Picture Cards

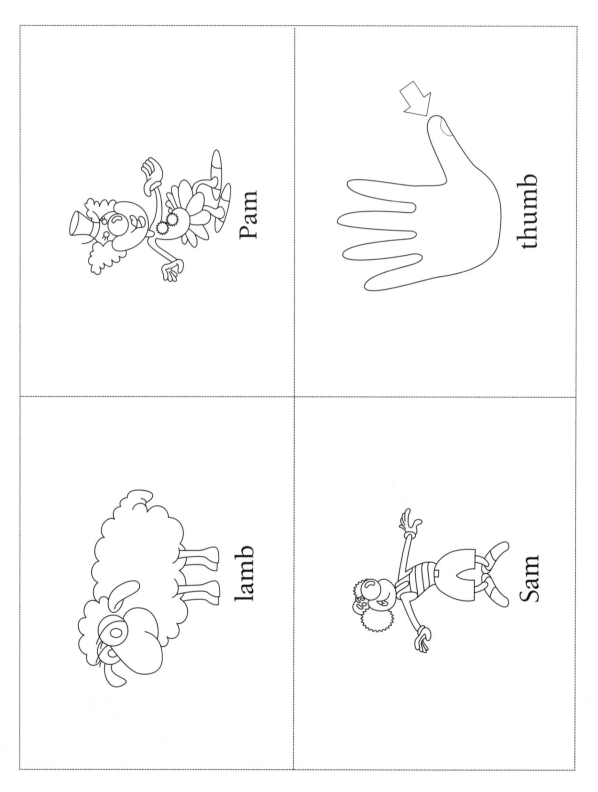

Pam

thumb

lamb

Sam

Picture Cards

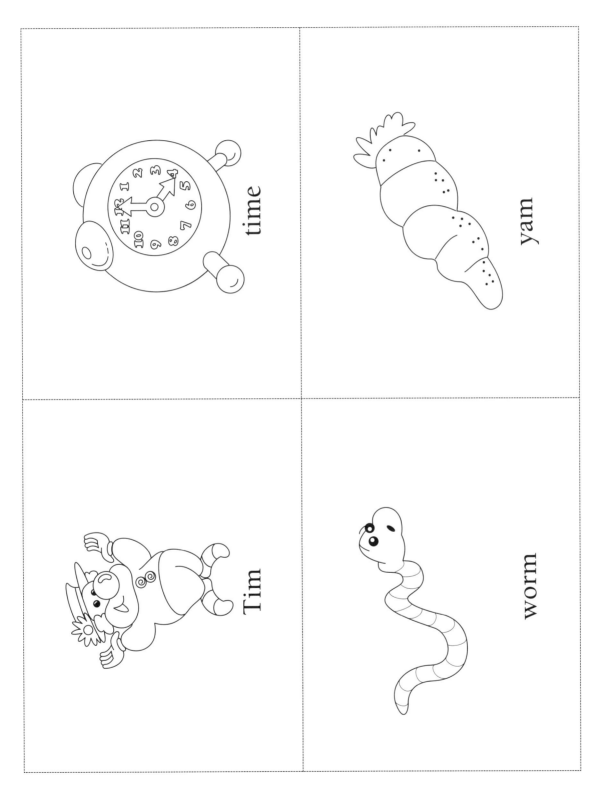

time

yam

Tim

worm

Picture Cards

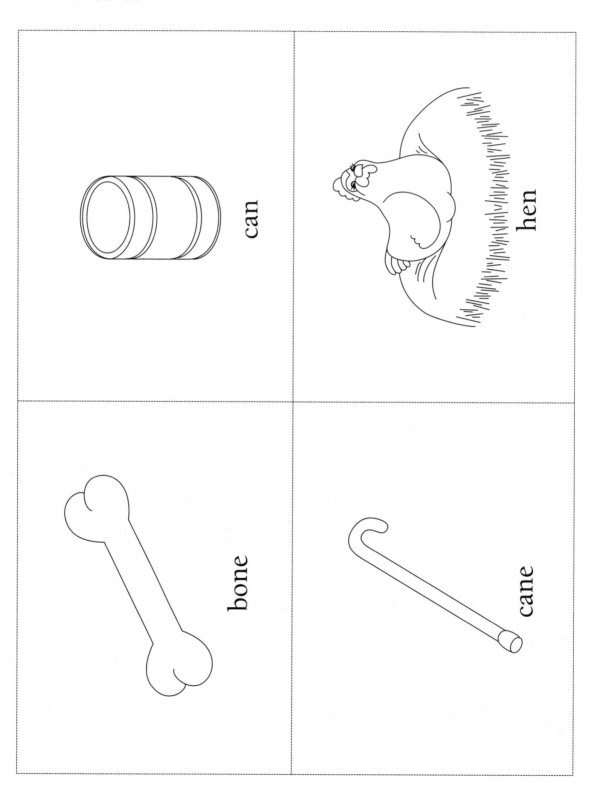

can

hen

bone

cane

Picture Cards

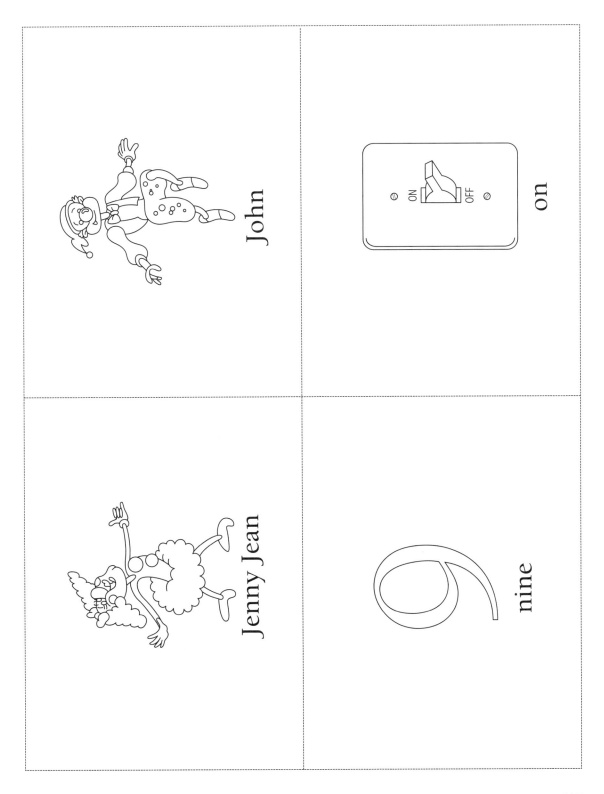

John

on

Jenny Jean

nine

Picture Cards

pan

ten

one

sun

Word Count Lists

Final /m/		Final /n/	
Word	**Frequency**	**Word**	**Frequency**
blam	1	an	1
bottom	2	been	1
drum	1	between	1
from	3	can	1
gum	2	cane	4
ham	5	chin	2
him	2	clown	10
lamb	2	down	2
name	3	even	1
Pam	10	fun	7
plum	2	green	2
Sam	5	hen	4
scream	1	in	2
some	1	insane	1
team	1	Jenny Jean	4
thumb	2	John	5
Tim	5	nine	2
time	1	on	8
wham	1	one	1
worm	2	pan	1
yam	2	scene	1
		seen	1
		ten	2
		then	2
		when	3
Total Words: 54		**Total Words: 69**	

Picture Card Lists

Final /m/		Final /n/	
drum	Sam	bone	nine
gum	thumb	can	on
ham	Tim	cane	one
him	time	hen	pan
lamb	worm	Jenny Jean	sun
Pam	yam	John	ten

Production Practice and Carryover Activities

- Make a **lamb**. Draw the shape of a **lamb on construction** paper. Glue **cotton** balls **on** the body.

- Chew **gum** and practice blowing bubbles.

- **Climb** on a slide or jungle **gym**.

- Eat a **plum** for a snack and say "**yum-yum**."

- Use a coffee **can** to make a **drum**. Have **children** beat it either **one**, **nine**, or **ten** times.

- Use play dough to make objects from the story (e.g., *worm*, *cane*, or *plum*).

- Cook pretend eggs in a **pan**. Count out **one**, **nine**, or **ten** eggs to put in the **pan**.

- Give directions to put objects or pictures **in** or **on** a **can**.

- Dress up and each take a **turn** acting like a **fun clown**.

- Draw a **clown** face on paper. Count out **ten** pieces of **yarn** and glue **them on** for hair.

Extension Activities

Rhyming

- Do these words rhyme? (yes or no)

ham - Sam	twine - twin
Tom - tomb	phone - bone
came - Kim	rain - run
home - roam	pan - man
worm - wham	down - done

- Which words rhyme?

one - bun - fine	sign - line - sun
can - cane - tan	rain - town - train
lime - time - Tim	clock - arm - alarm
hen - boom - room	him - whim - wham
worm - squirm - wiggle	ten - noon - cartoon

- Tell a word that rhymes with *gum, Pam, fame, beam, comb, sun, fin, brown, cone, can.*

Vocabulary Development

- Read the story and discuss vocabulary that may be new to students: *balance, cane, insane, yam, drum roll, lights go down, make a scene.*

Basic Concepts

- Show illustrations from the story or the individual sequence cards. Ask questions that require children to understand and use concept terms to respond. *Where is the ham? (on the cane) Where is the lamb? (on top) Where is the worm? (in the plum).*

- Have children stack real objects and show which items are on top and which are on the bottom.

Third-Person Singular Verbs

- Use illustrations from the story or sequence cards and ask questions to elicit third-person singular verb forms. *What happens to the egg? (drops) How does Jenny Jean get to the top? (climbs) What does the worm do? (chews gum) What does the crowd do? (claps, cheers)*

Critical Thinking

- Make predictions about what will happen if various objects are dropped on the floor. Will the objects break, bounce, or roll? What sound will you hear when it hits the floor? What would happen to the objects if they dropped in mud, in water, on a pillow, or on the carpet?

- Do experiments with a balance scale. Place individual objects or groups of objects on the scale. Predict which will be heavier or lighter.

Deep in the town
of Gulliver Gap,
a flock of sheep
woke up from their nap.

GULLIVER GAP

Rested and ready,
full of zip and some zap,
they felt like a trip
up top to Mount Tip Tap.

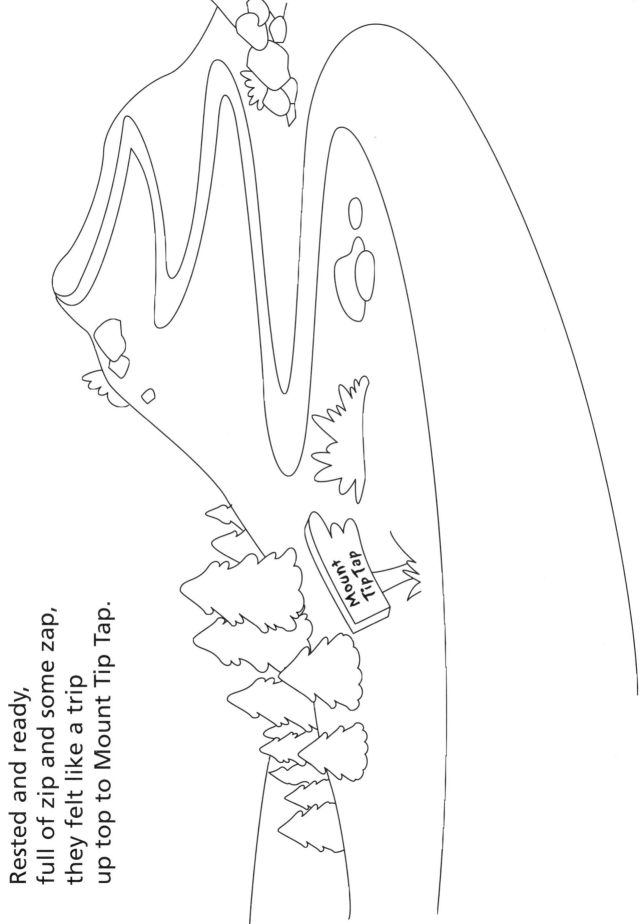

Mount Tip Tap

So the sheep, with a hop
and a clip, clap, clop,
climbed up and up
to the Mount Tip Tap top.

4

When they got
to the top
of the slope,
they did stop
to slurp on soup
and sip on some pop.

Deep in the town
of Gulliver Gap,
Pip had some rope
and a new silver snap.

She'd use her rope
with the new silver snap
to get to the tiptop
of ol' Mount Tip Tap.

So Pip, with her rope,
and a clip, clap, clop,
climbed up and up
to the Mount Tip Tap top.

As she got to the top,
Pip sat with the sheep
and a cup of hot tea
on the slope so steep.

Deep in the town
of Gulliver Gap,
a Scout troop rode,
each one in a cap.

They let loose a "Whoop!"
and a clip, clap, clop,
then climbed up in their Jeep
to the Mount Tip Tap top.

Mount Tip Top

The horn honked a beep
and they came to a stop
as they joined the group
gathered on top.

The troop made flapjacks
in back of their Jeep
and set them on plates
for Pip and the sheep,
still slurping soup
and sipping on tea.
The top of Mount Tip Tap
was a sight to see!

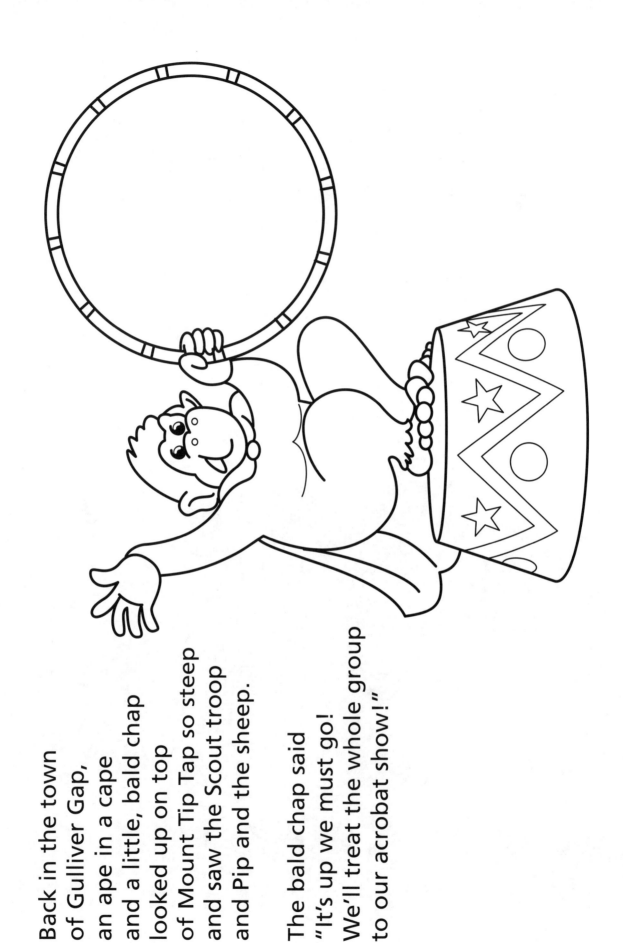

Back in the town
of Gulliver Gap,
an ape in a cape
and a little, bald chap
looked up on top
of Mount Tip Tap Tap so steep
and saw the Scout troop
and Pip and the sheep.

The bald chap said
"It's up we must go!
We'll treat the whole group
to our acrobat show!"

The bald chap and ape,
with a clip, clap, clop,
took their hoop up
to the Mount Tip Tap top.

The ape and the chap
did a flip through the hoop.
The soup-slurping sheep
did hand-stands for the group.
Then Pip and her rope
with the new silver snap
did a trick for the troop,
who started to clap.

19

At the end of the day
in Gulliver Gap,
Pip and her rope
and the bald-headed chap,
the ape with his hoop
and the troop waving caps
said goodbye to the sheep

as they clipped

and they clapped

and they clopped

past the Jeep.

GULLIVER GAP

20

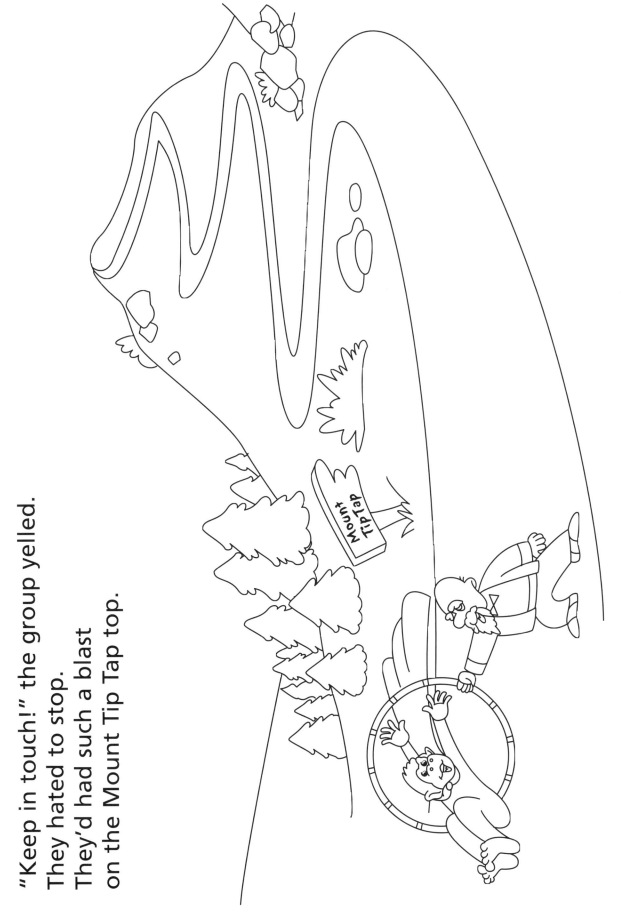

"Keep in touch!" the group yelled.
They hated to stop.
They'd had such a blast
on the Mount Tip Tap top.

Sequence Cards

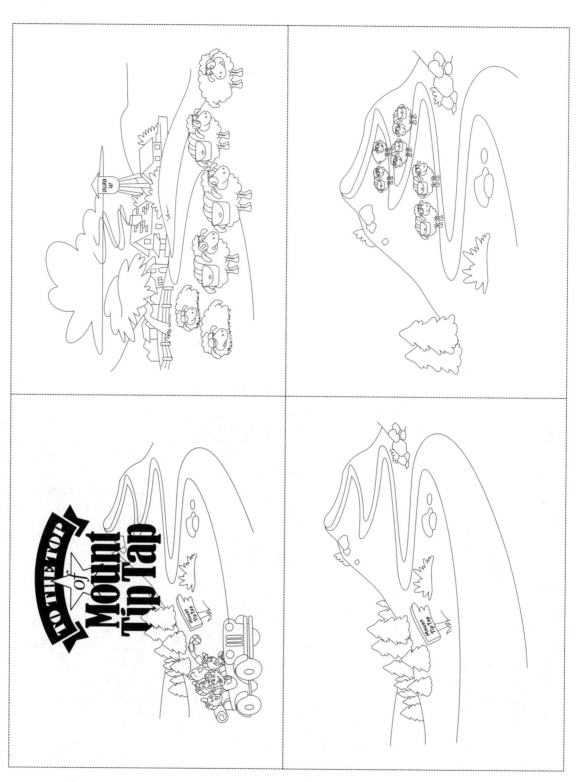

Sequence Cards

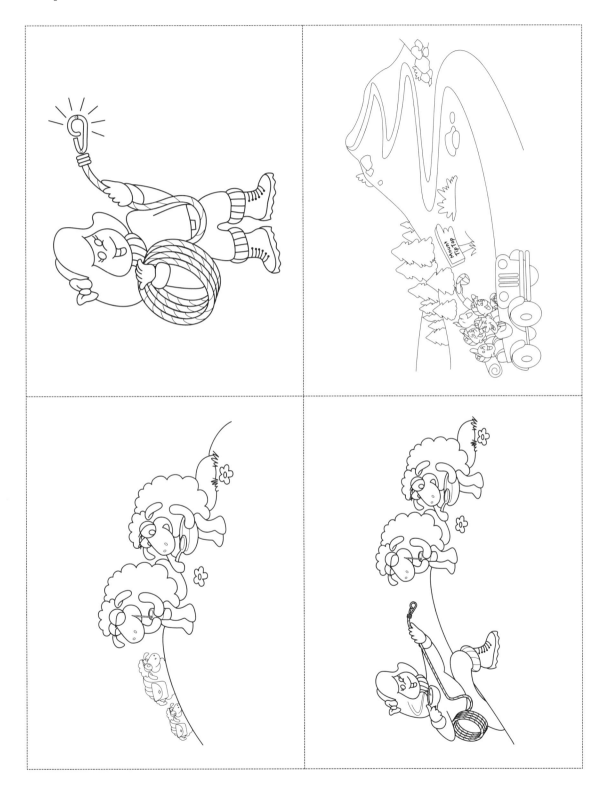

Sequence Cards

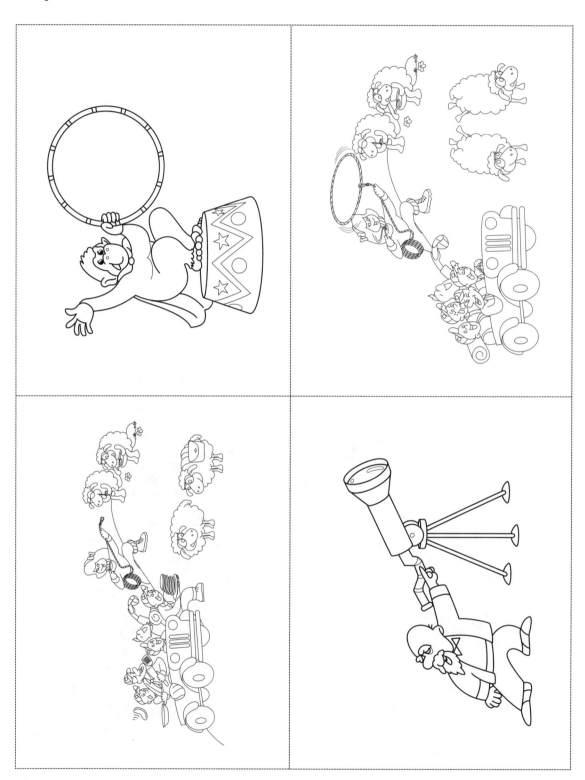

Sequence Cards

Picture Cards

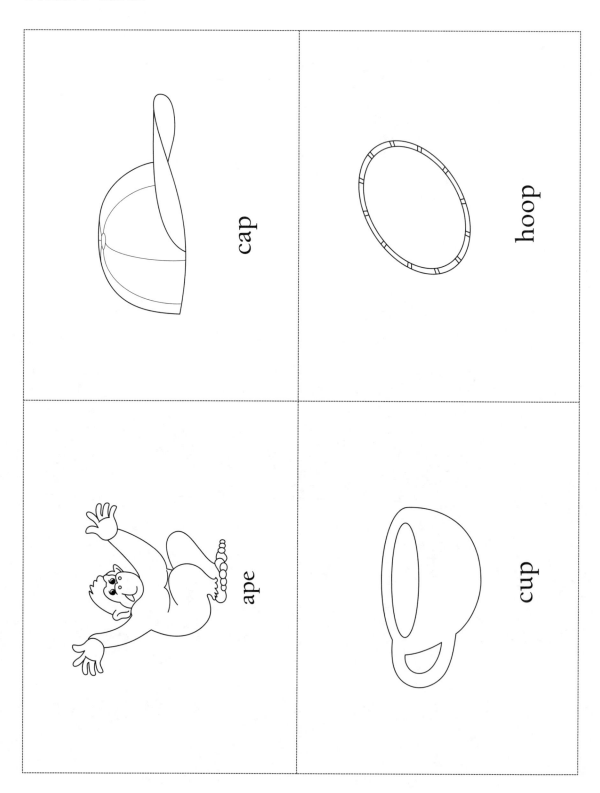

cap

hoop

ape

cup

Picture Cards

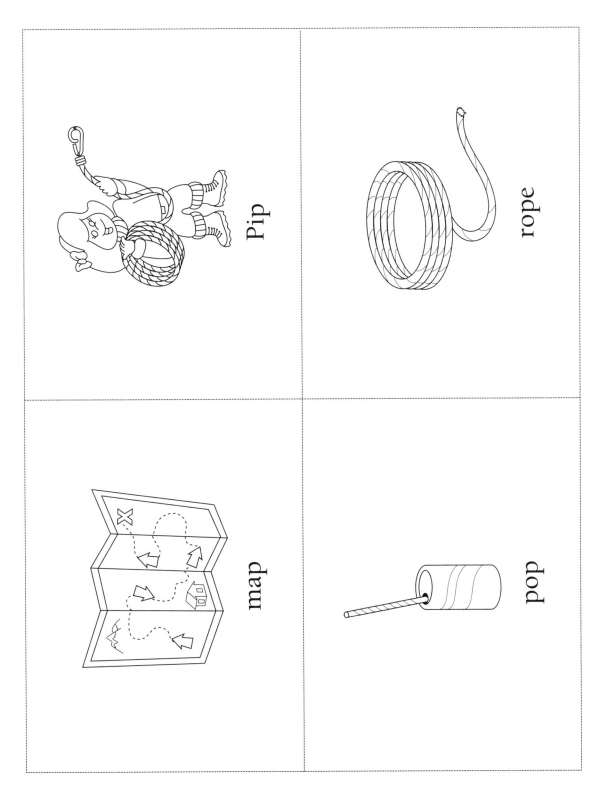

Pip

rope

map

pop

Picture Cards

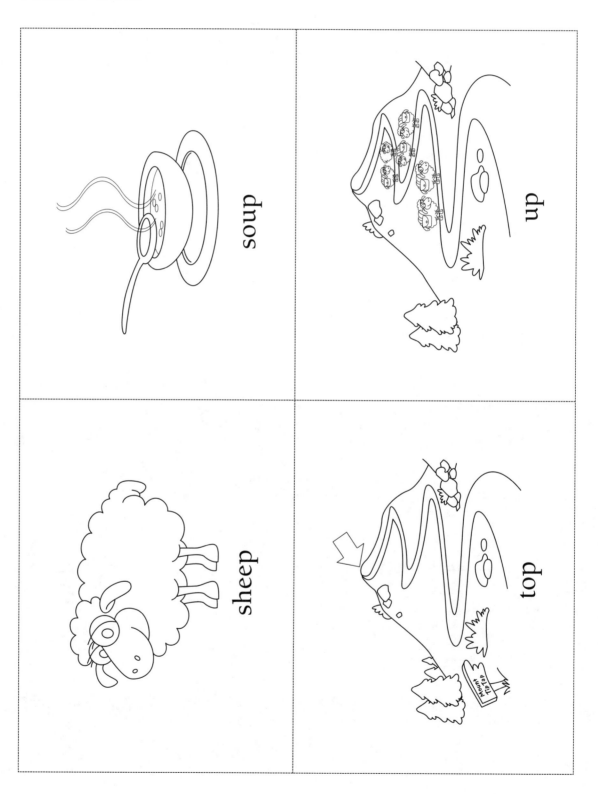

soup

up

sheep

top

Word Count List

Final /p/	
Word	**Frequency**
ape	4
beep	1
cap	1
cape	1
chap	5
clap	5
clip	4
clop	4
cup	1
deep	3
flip	1
Gap	5
group	4
hoop	3
hop	1
Jeep	3
keep	1
nap	1
Pip	7
pop	1
rope	5
sheep	7
sip	1
slope	2
slurp	1
snap	3
soup	3
steep	2
stop	3
Tap	9
Tip/tip	9
top	11
trip	1
troop	5
up	10
whoop	1
zap	1
zip	1
Total Words: 132	

Picture Card List

Final /p/
ape
cap
cup
hoop
map
Pip
pop
rope
sheep
soup
top
up

Production Practice and Carryover Activities

- Do tricks with a **hoop**. **Step** through it. Lay it on the floor and jump inside it. Toss a **cap** through it. Hula-**Hoop** with it.

- Make **soup** and eat it out of a **cup**.

- **Sip pop** in a **cup**.

- Use a **step** stool as Mount **Tip Tap**. Climb to the **top** and **drop** pictures into a **cap**. When all the pictures have been dropped, name the pictures that went into the **cap** and those that missed the **cap**.

- Lay cards on the floor in the **shape** of a mountain. **Hop** next to each picture to get to the **top**. **Hop** down the other side.

- Hide the cards around the room. **Tip**-toe around the room to find them, and pick them **up**.

- Play jump **rope**.

- Turn pictures facedown on a table. Use a pancake turner to **flip** the pictures over and name them.

- Blow bubbles and **pop** them.

- Glue cotton balls on a picture of a **sheep**. Make several sheep and put them all together to make a herd on **top** of Mount **Tip Tap**.

Extension Activities

Rhyming

- Do these words rhyme? (yes or no)

cap - tip	Jeep - dip
sheep - deep	gap - clap
slope - hope	Pip - rope
steep - shop	ape - tape
hoop - soup	pop - top

- Which words rhyme?

gap - cap - cape	snap - hoop - map
Pip - rope - soap	ape - sip - tape
sheep - ship - peep	clip - clop - pop
drape - drop - cop	steep - soup - coop
hype - pipe - hip	cup - pup - cap

- Tell a word that rhymes with *hip, hope, tape, clap, soup, mop, beep, drop, type, pup.*

Vocabulary Development

- Read the story and discuss vocabulary that may be new to students: *gap, herd, slope, steep, flapjacks, chap, acrobat, troop, full of zip and zap.*

- After talking about the meaning of the words *herd* and *troop,* point out that there are other words used to identify specific groups — *pack of wolves, school of fish, flock of birds, litter of puppies, pride of lions,* and *gaggle of geese.*

Past Tense Verbs

- Use the story or sequence cards to elicit both regular and irregular past tense verbs by asking what the different characters did: *climbed, slurped, sipped, honked, looked, flipped, clapped, woke, felt, sat, stood, came, made, set, saw, took, did, said.*

Critical Thinking

- Present children with pictures of a variety of items to consider taking on a mountain climbing trip. Have children decide which would be appropriate and explain why they did or didn't choose the items.

Rat·a·tat·tat
a Toot
a Twect

With my white hat and suit
and a steady drum beat,
we look right and left,
then start moving our feet.

With a rat-a-tat-tat
and a toot and a tweet,
my marching band starts
to step on the street.

What is the pounding
in line behind me?
My friends Brett and Chet
hit drums mightily.

With a rat-a-tat-tat
and a toot and a tweet,
we march right along,
my friends keeping beat.

Behind Brett and Chet
is a cat playing flute,
followed by Kate
in a float made of fruit.

With a rat-a-tat-tat
and a toot and a tweet,
my marching band marches
along in the street.

After Kate in a float
and a cat playing flute
and Brett and Chet drumming
and me in my suit
is a goat with a talent
exceedingly rare:
He juggles a pot
and eight pans in the air.

With a rat-a-tat-tat
and a toot and a tweet,
we keep marching on
in spite of the heat.

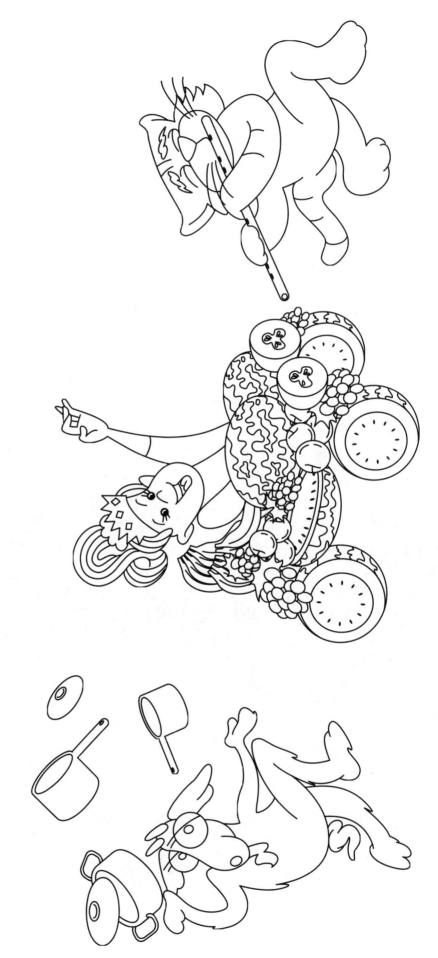

A gnat and a newt
with their tubas go "BLAT!"
in line behind Kate
and the goat and the cat,
while Brett and Chet
and me in the lead
are starting to feel
quite warm indeed.

With a rat-a-tat-tat
and a toot and a tweet,
our marching slows down
to a stop in the street.

The pot-juggling goat
the gnat, the newt,
Kate, the cat
(still tooting her flute),
me, the drummers
(my friends Brett and Chet)
can march no longer
in the heat and the sweat.

At the instant we wave
goodbye to the crowd,
the hot sun is blocked
by a fat, little cloud.

That fat, little cloud
is full of relief,
and sweet rain falls down
to the hot, hot street.

So...

With a rat-a-tat-tat
and a toot and a tweet,
the newt and the gnat
blow "BLAT!" in the street.

The goat with the talent
exceedingly rare
juggles his pot
and eight pans in the air.

With rain coming down,
the cat blows her flute
and Kate rides the float
made out of fruit.

My friends Brett and Chet
hit the drums with a beat.
Our fat, little cloud
helped us all beat the heat!

Sequence Cards

Sequence Cards

Sequence Cards

Sequence Cards

Picture Cards

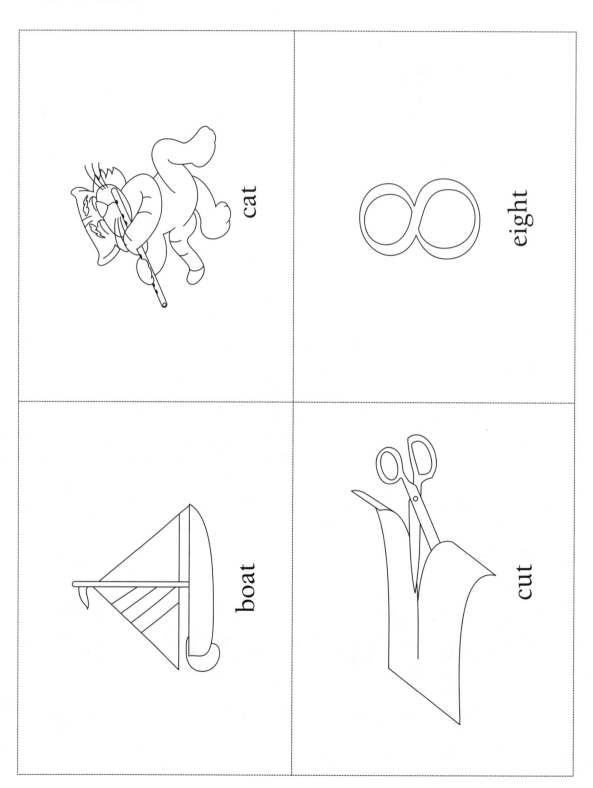

cat

eight

boat

cut

Picture Cards

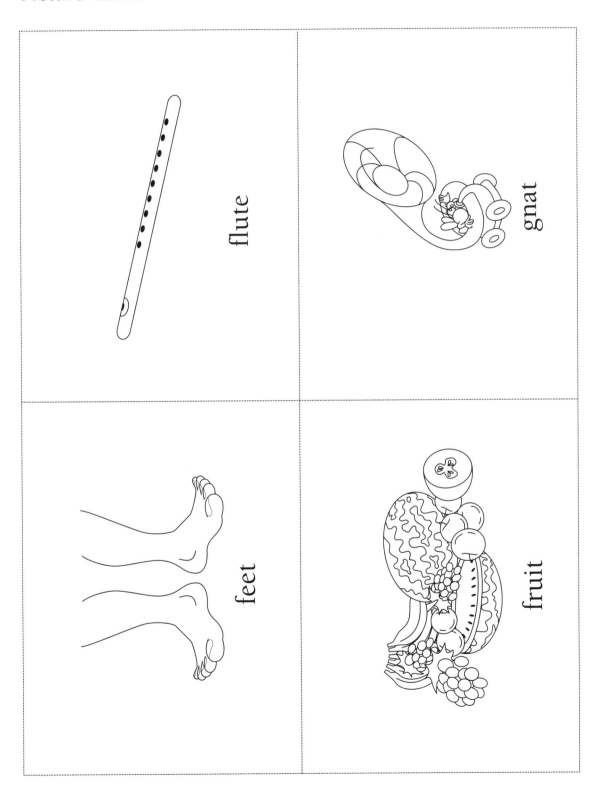

flute

gnat

feet

fruit

Picture Cards

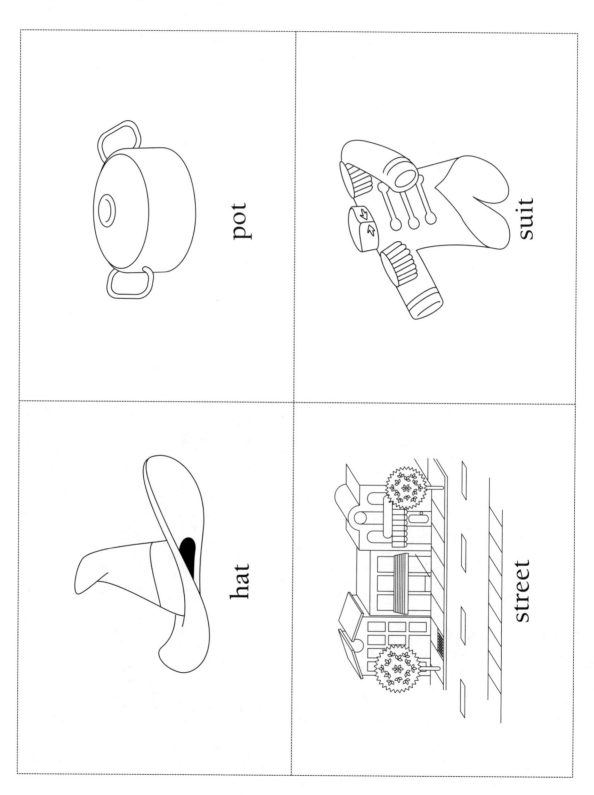

pot

suit

hat

street

Word Count List

Final /t/

Word	Frequency
at	1
beat	4
blat	2
Brett	6
cat	5
Chet	6
eight	2
fat	3
feet	1
float	3
flute	4
fruit	2
gnat	3
goat	4
hat	1
heat	3
hit	2
hot	3
Kate	5
newt	3
pot	3
quite	1
rat	6
right	2
spite	1
street	5
suit	2
sweat	1
sweet	1
tat	12
that	1
toot	6
tweet	6
what	1
white	1

Total Words: 112

Picture Card List

Final /t/

boat
cat
cut
eight
feet
flute
fruit
gnat
hat
pot
street
suit

Production Practice and Carryover Activities

- Make a **street** using tape (or chalk outside). Place picture cards in line next to the **street**. March down the **street** and name the pictures as you go past them.

- Measure the **street** and see how many **feet** long **it** is.

- Classify foods as **fruit** or **not fruit**.

- Pull pictures **out** of a **pot** or **hat** and label them.

- Toss pictures into a **hat**. Use short phrases to tell **what** is in the **hat** (e.g., **cat** in the **hat**; **feet** in the **hat**).

- Make a parade **hat** or **suit**.

- Stomp a **beat** with your **feet** and have children **imitate it**.

- Pretend you are playing instruments in a marching band. Children choose the instrument they want to play and say the noise their instrument makes while marching (e.g., **blat** for tubas, **tweet** or **toot** for flutes, or **rat-a-tat-tat** for drums).

- Lay picture cards on the floor randomly. Have children take turns giving you or peers directions for where to go when they reach each picture (e.g., left, **right**, or **straight**).

- **Sit** on chairs and pretend each child is in a **boat**. Place pictures on both the **right** and left sides of the chair. Have the children go fishing for the pictures they see **float** in the water. Give specific directions to catch something on the left or **right**. Have children tell you what they **caught** and on which side **it** was.

Extension Activities

Rhyming

- Do these words rhyme? (yes or no)

hat - cat	flute - fruit
boat - float	fat - fit
bite - fight	blat - newt
hot - hit	Kate - date
seat - sit	Brett - Chet

- Which words rhyme?

Chet - Brett - nut	boat - bite - fight
hat - sit - cat	cut - wheat - what
kite - Kate - mate	pit - hit - pet
hot - heat - feet	note - float - not
newt - night - suit	cute - pot - cot

- Tell a word that rhymes with *night, beat, fat, sit, boat, hot, hate, pet, boot, cut.*

Vocabulary Development

- Read the story and discuss vocabulary that may be new to students: *talent, gnat, newt, tuba, juggle, in spite of, full of relief.*

Absurdities

- Present individual sequence cards and talk to students about the absurdities in the pictures. *Do cats really play flutes? Why not? Why is a gnat playing a tuba silly? Can a goat juggle?* Help children think of other absurd things for animals to do.

Classification

- Classify real instruments or pictures of instruments. For younger children, sort them according to how you play them (e.g., hit them vs. blow into them). For older children, introduce the terms *woodwinds*, *percussion*, and *strings*.

Third-Person Singular Verbs

- Use illustrations from the story or sequence cards and ask questions to elicit third-person singular verb forms. *What does the goat do? (juggles) What does the band do? (marches) Tell me about Brett. (Brett hits the drum.) Tell me what Kate does. (Kate rides the float.)*

Critical Thinking

- Have children create their own instruments using a variety of common objects (e.g., boxes, plastic bowls, paper plates, cardboard tubes, beads, string, buttons, or paper). Think of names for the unique instruments, and have children tell or demonstrate how to play them.

Mack and The Yak Horn Stew

If you hike to the brook
and go past the lake,
just left of the dike
and a rusty brown rake,
a ramshackle shack
is what you will see,
where Mack the Ogre lives
with his cook, named Marie.

She decided to make
a fine stew for Mack
seasoned with salt
and the horn of a yak.

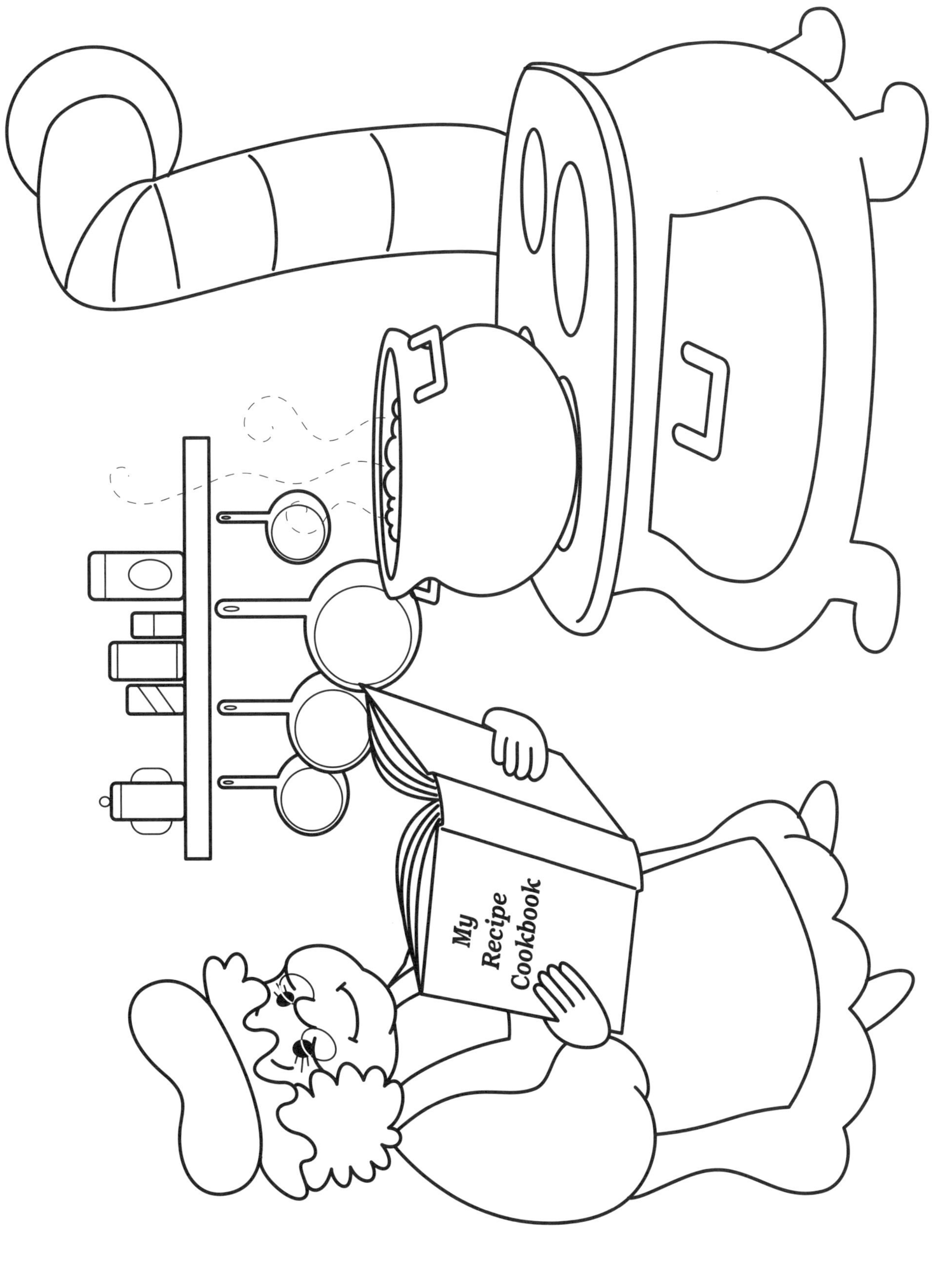
My
Recipe
Cookbook

Mack took a lick
from the stick in the pot.
Marie hoped he'd like
her yak stew a lot.

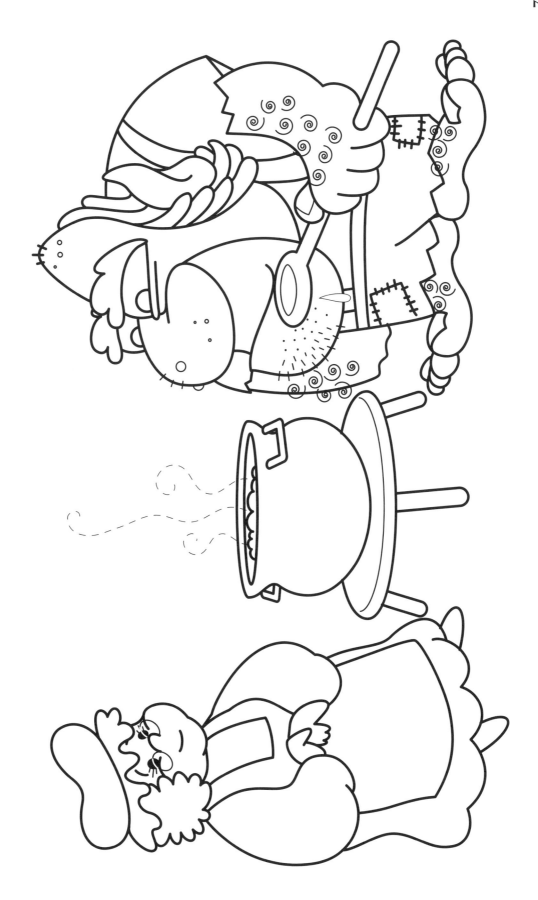

Instead Mack stuck out
his tongue and yelled, "YUK!"
He made a sick face
and spat out a "BLUCCH!"

"This stew that you make,
seasoned with salt
and the horn of a yak,
tastes perfectly awful.
Quick! Take it back!"

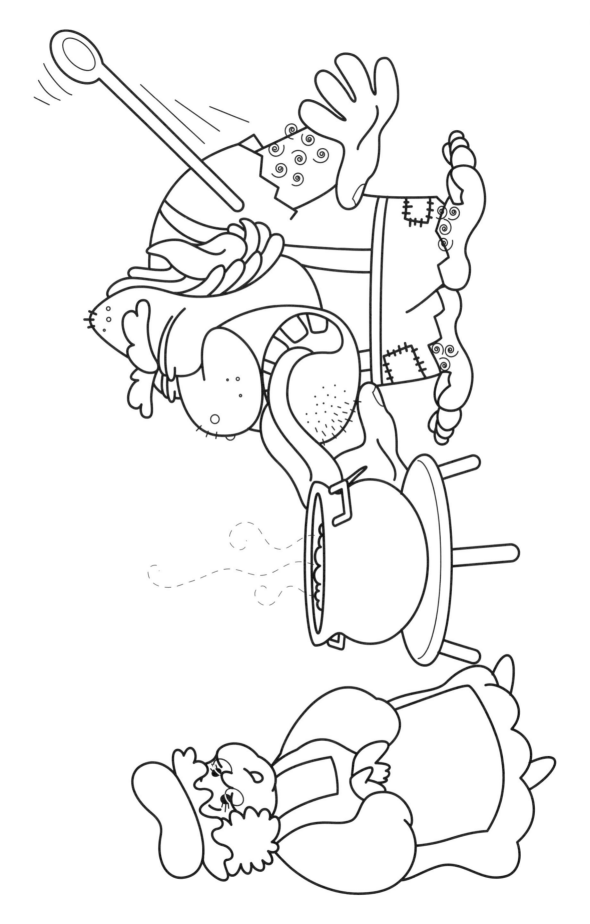

So Marie, Mack's cook,
walked back to her stove
and added a pinch of
black pepper and clove.

Marie stirred the stew.
She stirred it up quick,
then served it to Mack
on her thick stirring stick.

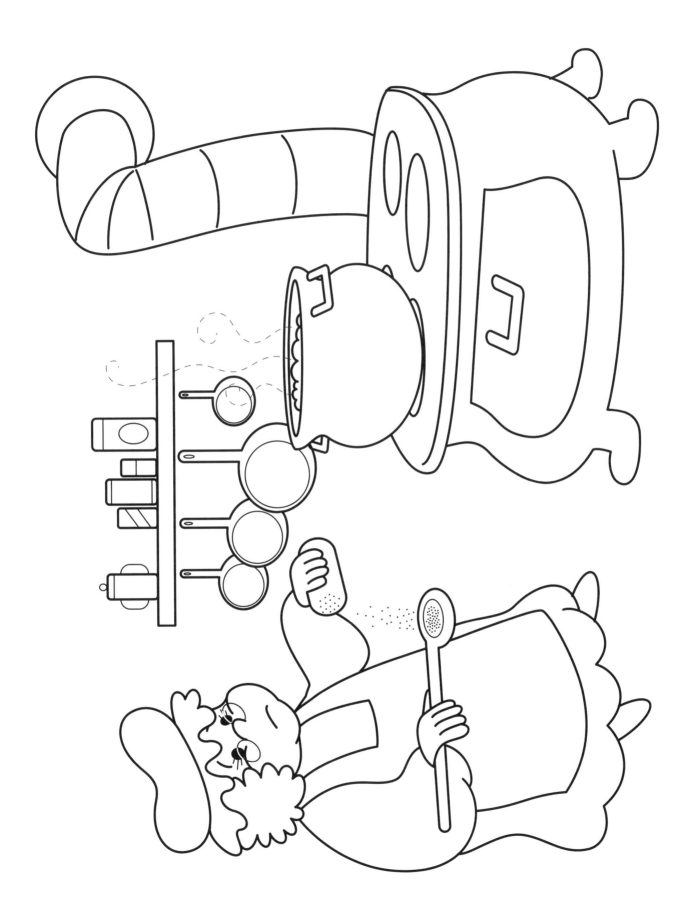

Mack took a lick
from the stick in the pot.
Marie was sure he'd like
her new stew a lot.

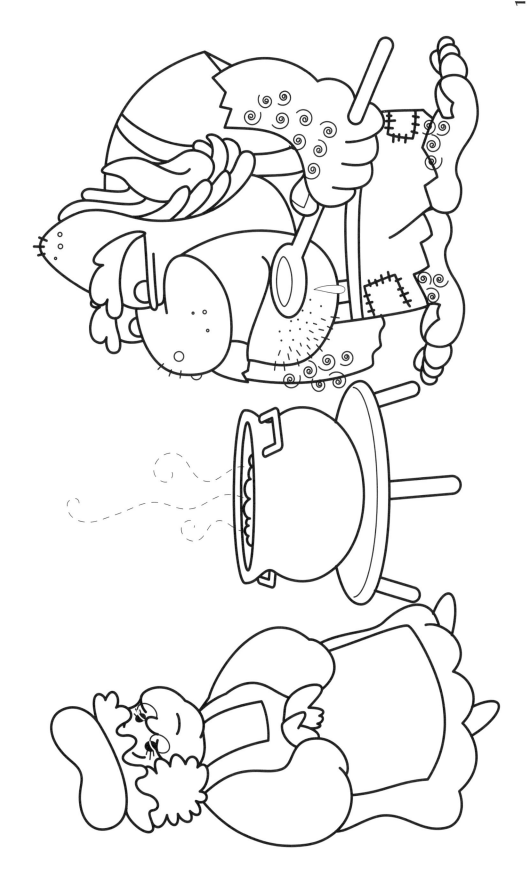

Instead Mack stuck out
his tongue and yelled, "YUK!"
He made a sick face
and spat out a "BLUCCH!"

"This stew that you cook
back there on your stove
with a pinch of black pepper
and a dash of some clove,
seasoned with salt
and the horn of a yak
tastes perfectly awful.
Quick! Take it back!"

14

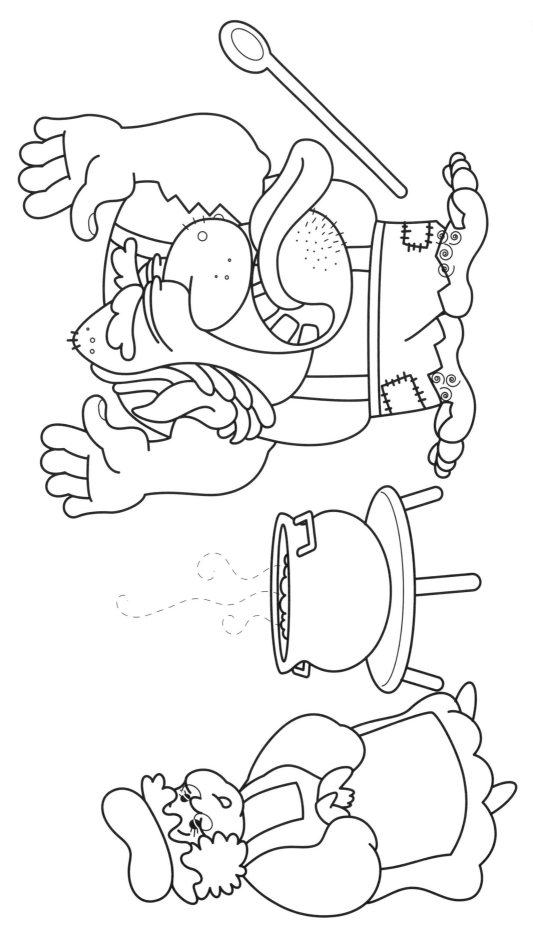

So Marie returned
to her kitchen to find
a sack of big onions
and a spice of some kind.

"These things should help
the flavor improve."
She thought to herself,
"Mack will approve."

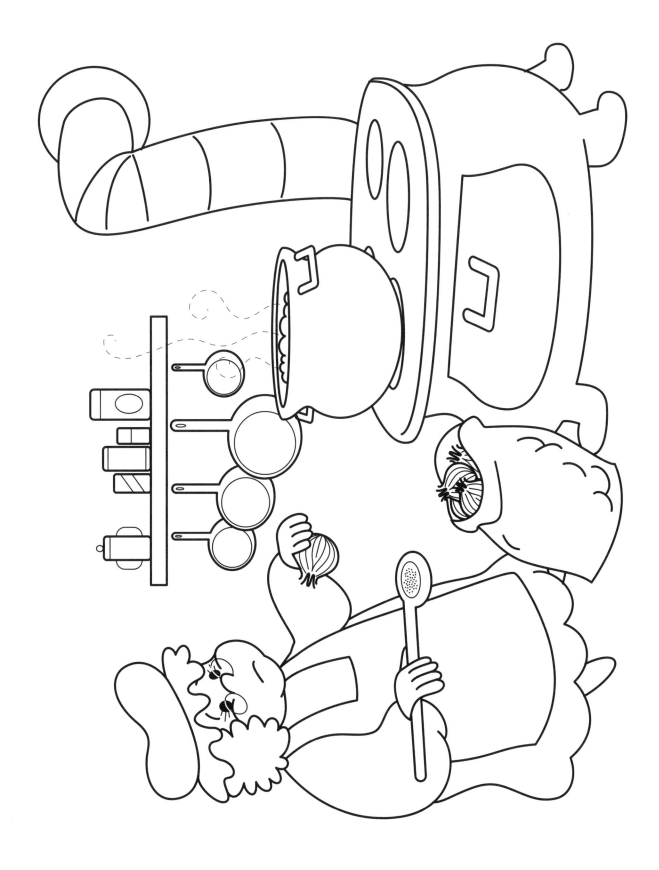

And then Mack yelled back...

"Adding the onions
and a spice of some kind
makes it taste even worse.
What else can you find?

I don't like this stew
cooked on your stove
with a pinch of black pepper
and a dash of some clove,
seasoned with salt
and the horn of a yak.
It's perfectly awful.
Quick! Take it back!"

But as Mack took a lick
from Marie's stirring stick
The result was the same—
the stew made him sick!

Once more Mack stuck out
his tongue and yelled, "Yuk!"
He made a sick face
and spat out a "BLUCCH!"

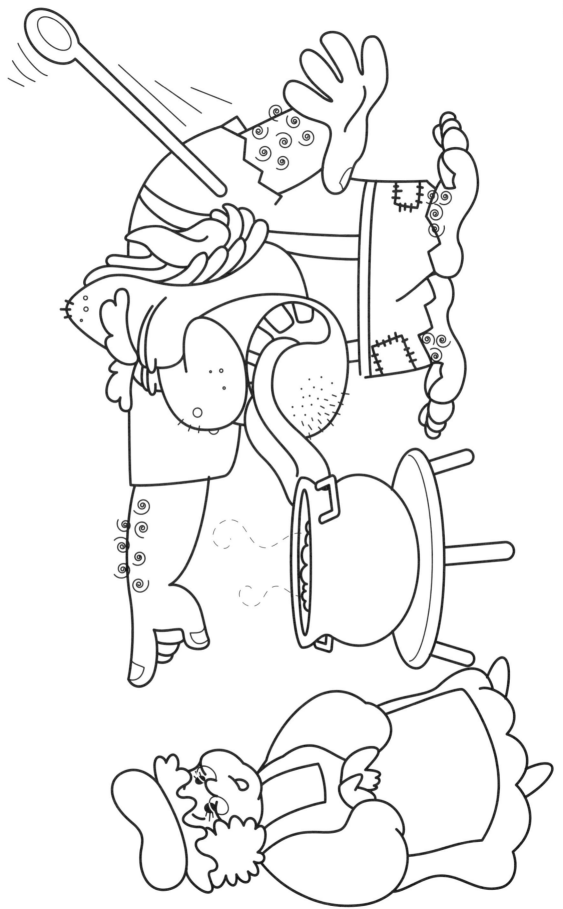

Marie had no idea
of what she could do.
What could she use
to improve her stew?

Marie was distracted
and forgot to duck.
She knocked down a shelf—
What terrible luck!

A basket that held
Mack's dirty clothes
fell into the stew,
splashing her nose.

Out came a shirt
and a stinky, old sock.
The clothes tumbled out
and fell into the crock.

"Oh my!" gasped Marie.
"What on earth shall I do?"
But Mack was still hungry
and demanded his stew.

So she served him the stew
with the stinky, old clothes.
It stunk so bad,
she held her nose.

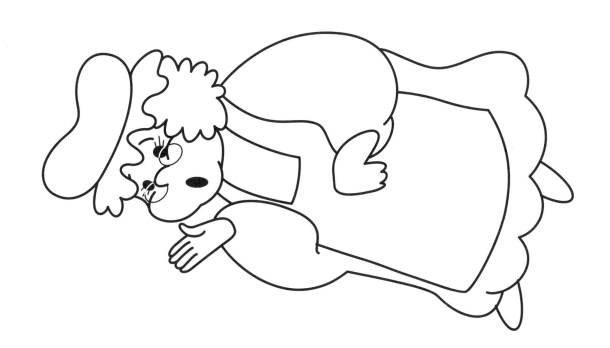

She had served it with onions
and some kind of spice.
That time she was sure
her stew would taste nice.

She'd cooked and stirred
the stew on her stove
with a pinch of black pepper
and a dash of some clove.

She'd seasoned with salt
and the horn of a yak,
but Mack spat and sputtered
and sent it right back.

But this time...

Mack took a lick
from the stick in the pot
And declared very loudly—

"I LIKE THIS STEW A LOT!"

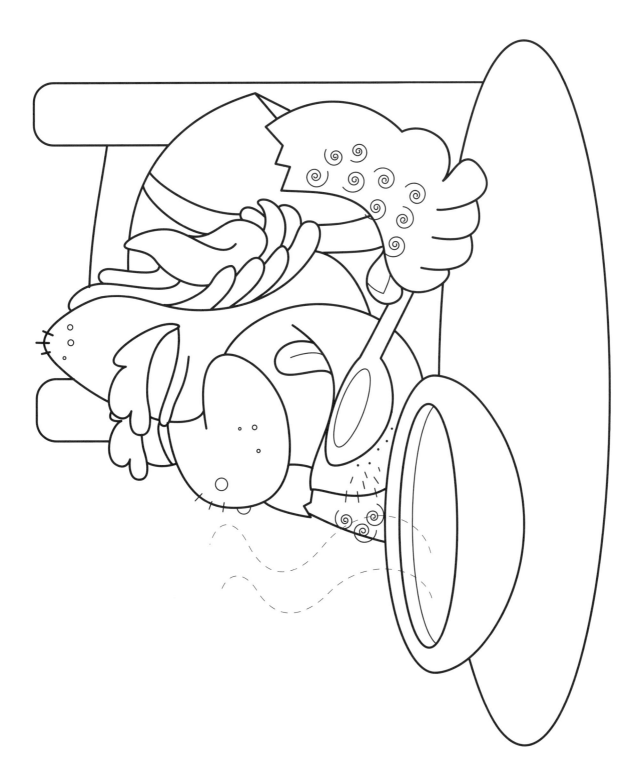

Sequence Cards

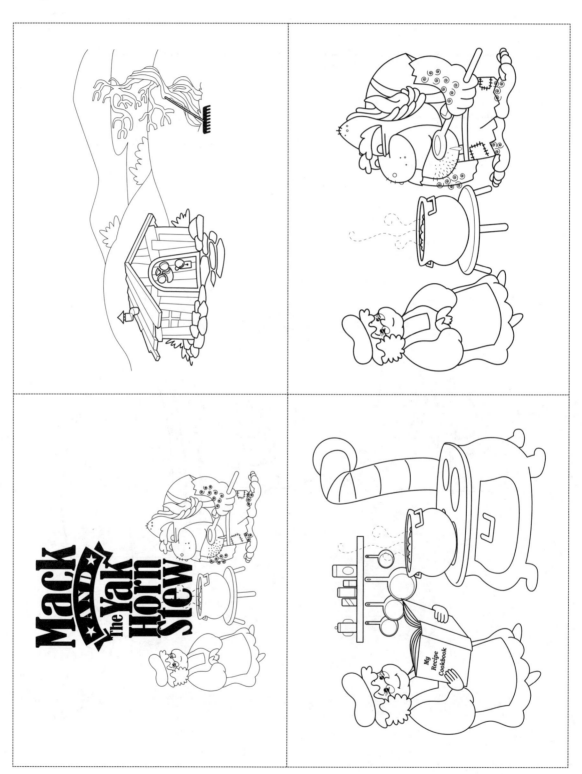

Sequence Cards

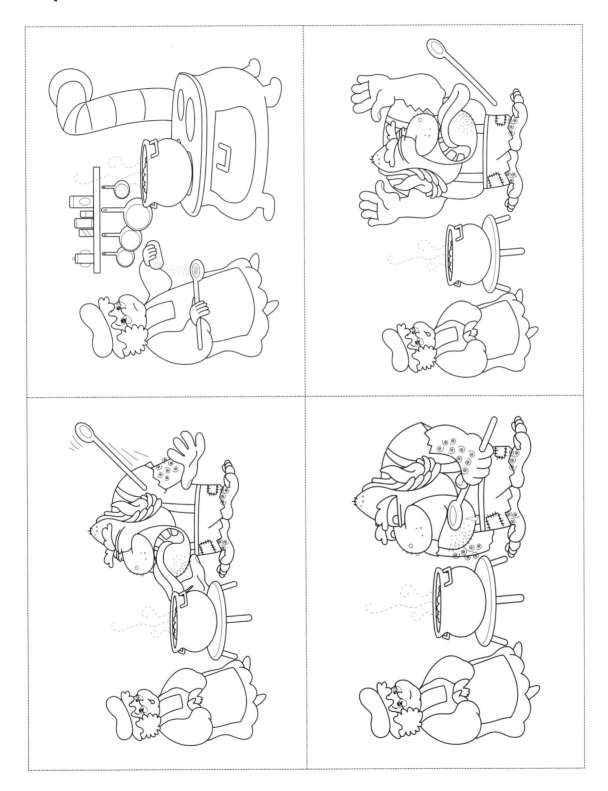

Sequence Cards

Sequence Cards

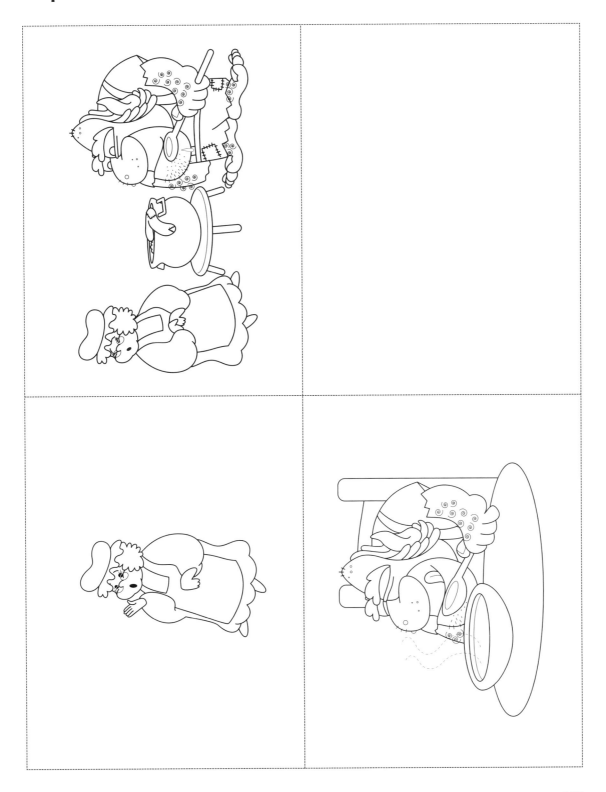

Picture Cards

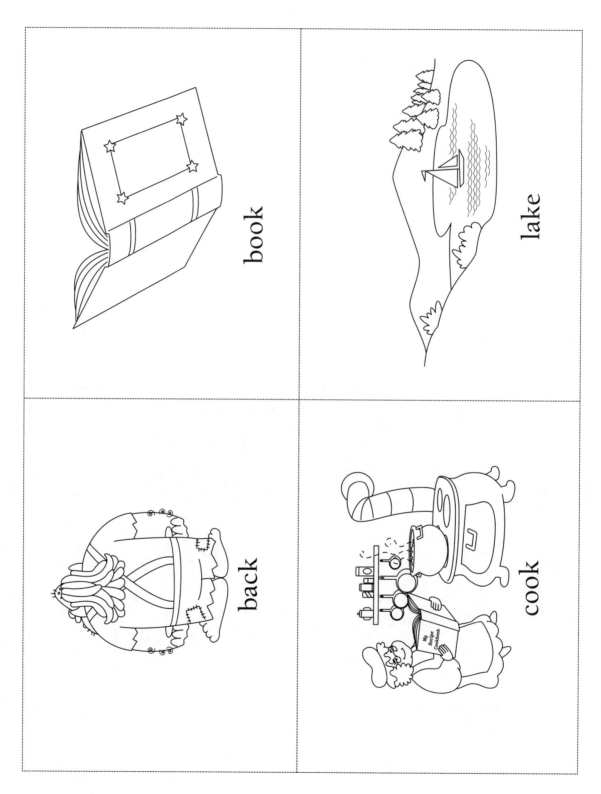

book

lake

back

cook

Picture Cards

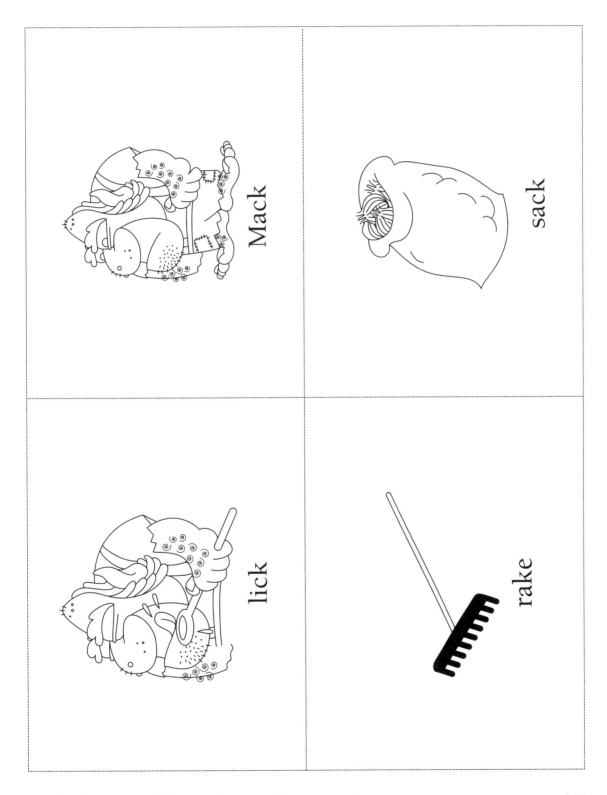

Mack

sack

lick

rake

Picture Cards

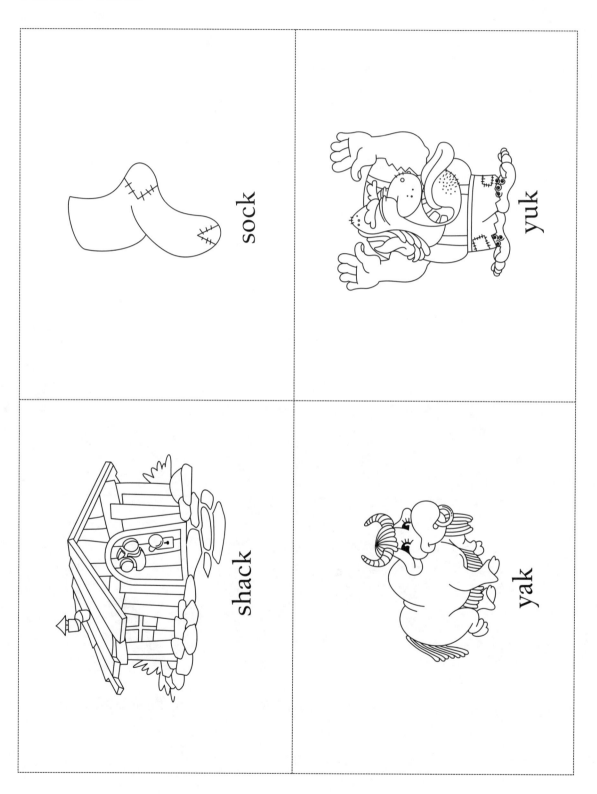

sock

yuk

shack

yak

Word Count List

Final /k/	
Word	**Frequency**
back	7
black	4
blucch	3
brook	1
cook	3
crock	1
dike	1
duck	1
hike	1
lake	1
lick	4
like	4
luck	1
Mack	14
make	2
quick	4
rake	1
sack	1
shack	1
sick	4
sock	1
stick	5
stuck	3
take	3
thick	1
took	4
yak	6
yuk	3

Total Words: 85

Picture Card List

Final /k/
back
book
cook
lake
lick
Mack
rake
sack
shack
sock
yak
yuk

Production Practice and Carryover Activities

- Pretend you are going to **cook** for **Mack**. Tell what you will **cook** for him.

- Pick real objects or pictures out of a **sack** and name them.

- Give each child a **sock** to **make** puppets of **Mack** and Marie. Act out the story.

- Show pictures of different kinds of food. Have children group foods as those that you **cook** or those that you don't **cook**.

- Cut out pictures of foods and glue them on sheets of **black** paper. Staple sheets together to make a **cookbook**.

- Put objects (e.g., plastic foods or absurd items) or picture cards in a **crock** to **make** stew for **Mack**. Stir it with a stirring **stick** (e.g., large wooden spoon). Tell what things **Mack** will **like** or not **like** in the stew.

- **Lick** Popsicles or **suck** on suckers.

- Create a trail of picture cards and **take** a **hike** or **walk** to find them. Collect the pictures in a **backpack**. Tell what pictures were found when you return.

- Go fishing for pictures. Put paper clips on individual picture cards. Place picture cards together in a pretend **lake** or **brook**. Use a **stick** (or similar object) with a magnet attached by a string to **pick** up the pictures.

Extension Activities

Rhyming

- Do these words rhyme? (yes or no)

back - crack	brook - black
cook - book	crock - dike
yuk - yak	sack - shack
lick - tick	peek - pick
sick - sock	rake - snake

- Which words rhyme?

make - bake - cook	bike - Mack - back
took - lake - look	black - snack - book
peek - yak - sneak	wick - tick - tock
stuck - hike - yuk	quick - lock - dock
woke - cake - poke	luck - duck - neck

- Tell a word that rhymes with *Mack, cook, weak, poke, lock, rake, duck, hike, sick, shack.*

Vocabulary Development

- Read the story and discuss vocabulary that may be new to students: *dike, ramshackle, ogre, yak, seasoned, clove, flavor, approve, result, distracted, crock, a pinch, a dash.*

Attributes

- Set up a tasting party with various foods (e.g., soup, lemons, pretzels, cottage cheese, ice cream). Have children describe how the foods taste and feel (e.g., hot, sour, salty, lumpy, cold).

Multiple-Meaning Words

- Discuss words in the story that have multiple meanings: *pinch, dash, horn, yak, duck, sock, season, stick, serve, pepper.*

Possessives

- Use the storybook illustrations or sequence cards to talk about items and who their owners are. Elicit various possessive forms with models and direct questions. *Whose shack is this? (Mack's shack, his shack). The stove belongs to Marie. Whose stove is it? (hers, Marie's stove).*

Critical Thinking

- Cook two different types of soup (e.g., vegetable and chicken noodle, dry and canned). Compare and contrast the soups according to preparation, content, and taste. Have children tell which they like better and why.

It's time to go, Kelly and Kip!
Lock the door and come real quick.
And could you please
grab the keys?
Let's jump inside
and begin our ride
with our magic car in the country.

We see some crows dancing on cows.

Crows dance and kick.
Cows clap and lick.
Caw! Caw! Moo! Moo!
We all join in their whoop-ti-doo.
We call back
and wave our caps
from our magic car in the country.

A king and his cub are flying a kite.

"Keep it so high
way up in the sky!"
calls out the king
to the cub pulling string.
We drive beside
and watch kites glide
from our magic car in the country.

A cook is counting candles on cakes.

"1, 2, 3, 4, 5, 6,"
she counts and licks her hungry lips.
"All these cakes and candles, too,
keep birthday kids filled up. It's true."
We can't wait
to celebrate
with our magic car in the country.

Next we see calico cats in crimson coats.

They cuddle together
in the cold, chilly weather
on a cozy cot—
'til the sun gets hot.
They shed their coats
and ride on goats
toward our magic car in the country.

Candy canes and carnival games are at the top of the hill.

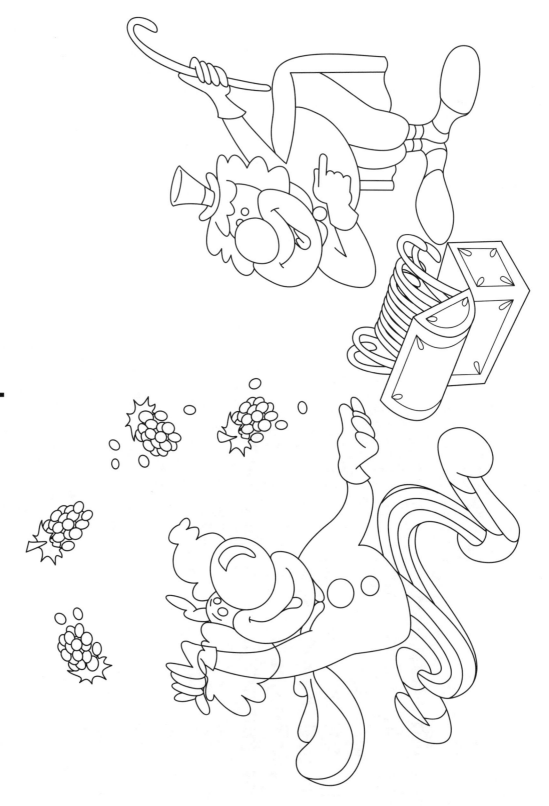

We crawl out to play
for the rest of the day,
while clowns in capes
juggle green grapes
and pull from cases
some canes and fun faces
for our magic car in the country.

Crack! Ka-boom!
Thunder claps and rain starts falling.

Kelly! Kip!
Come back quick!
The friends we met
are getting wet.
Pick them up on the way,
keep them dry and OK
with our magic car in the country.

"Who's first?" we cry
up toward the sky.
The clowns in capes
(still juggling grapes)
line up to ride
and pile inside
our magic car in the country.

"Who's next?" Kip asks.
It's calico cats!
They jump off goats
and don crimson coats.
As they load,
we hit the road
in our magic car in the country.

"Who now?" we call
as more drops fall.
The cook! The cake!
For goodness sake!
Collect your candles
and open the handle
to our magic car in the country.

"Who now?" we shout
with rain all about.
The king and his kite
come into sight,
with cub beside,
they come inside
our magic car in the country.

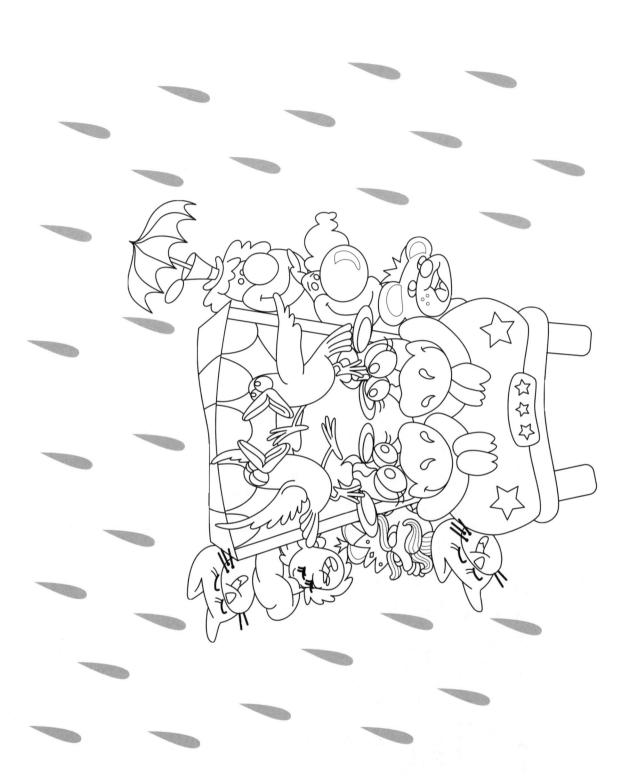

"Who's last?" we wonder
between claps of thunder.
"Caw! Caw! Moo! Moo!"
Crows and cows are on board, too.
As home we speed,
we're warm indeed
in our magic car in the country.

Come dry your toes,
all cows and crows
and kites and king
and cub pulling string.

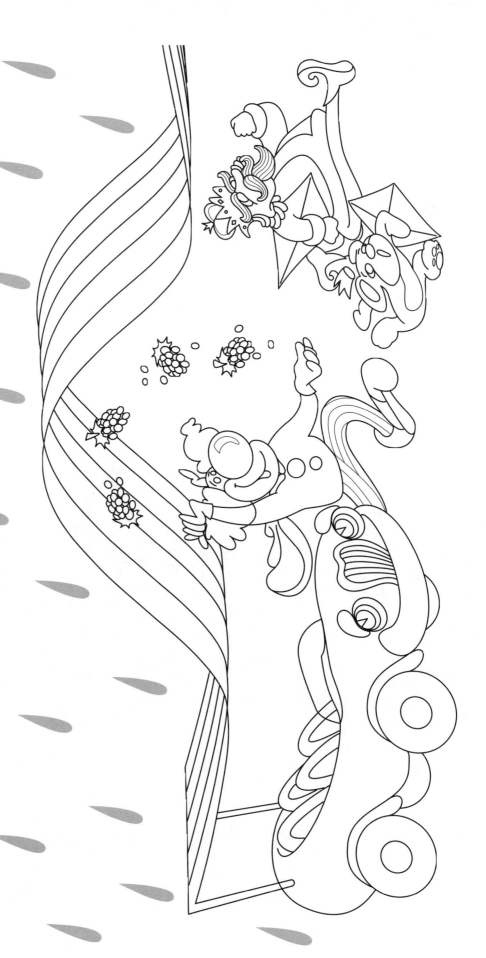

cats in coats
who rode on goats,
and clowns in capes
who juggle grapes.
Silly cook with a yummy treat,
cut the cake and let's all eat.

We're all wet,
but you can bet
a rainy day
can't stop our play.

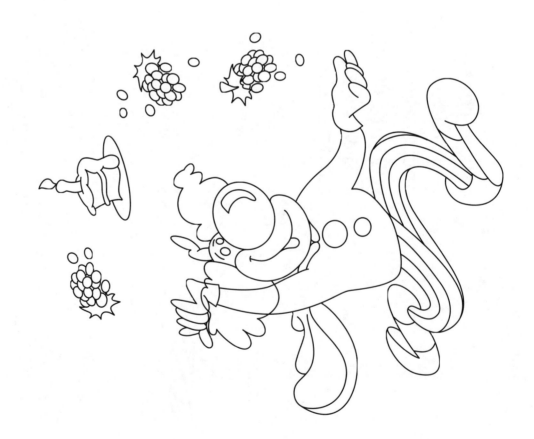

Here's our chance
to start a dance.
So give a big cheer
for who brought us here...

...our magic car

in the country!

Sequence Cards

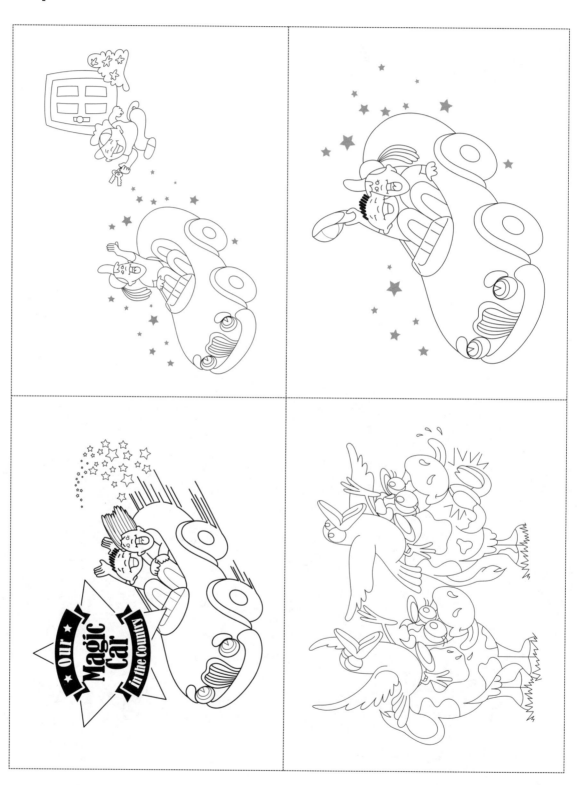

Sequence Cards

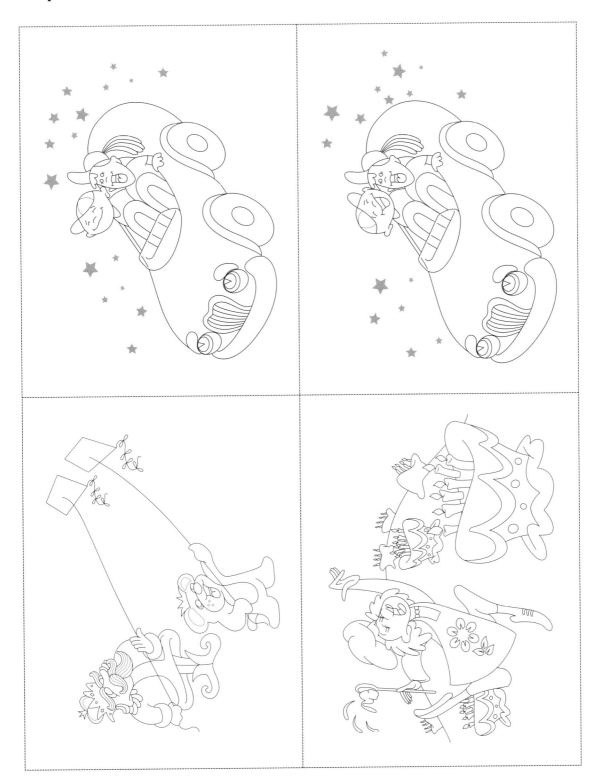

Sequence Cards

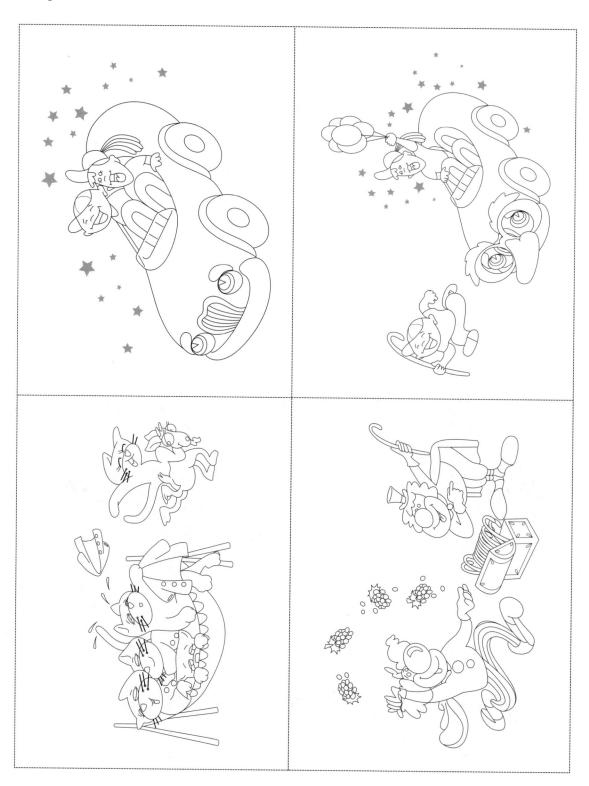

Sequence Cards

Sequence Cards

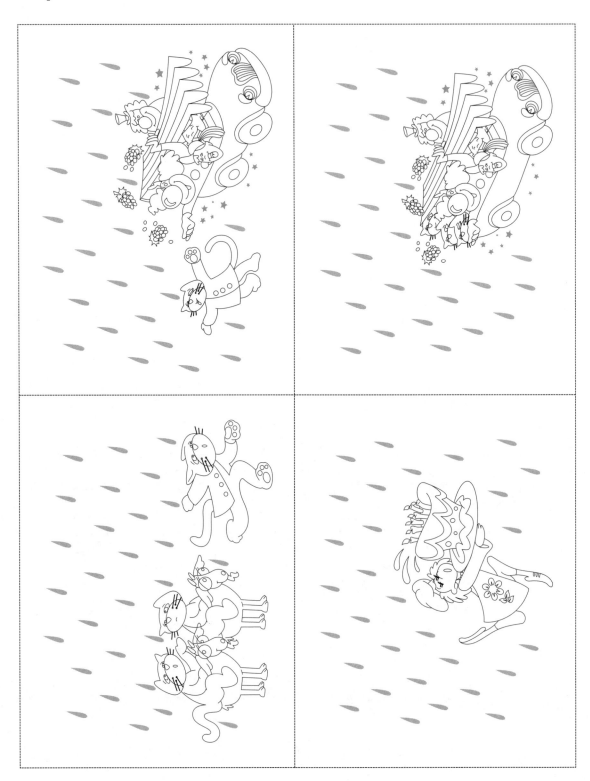

Sequence Cards

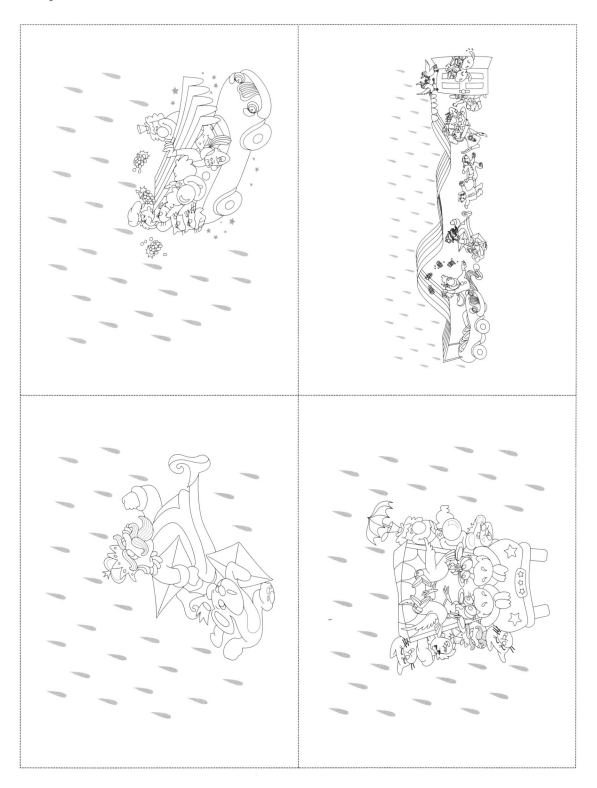

Sequence Cards

Picture Cards

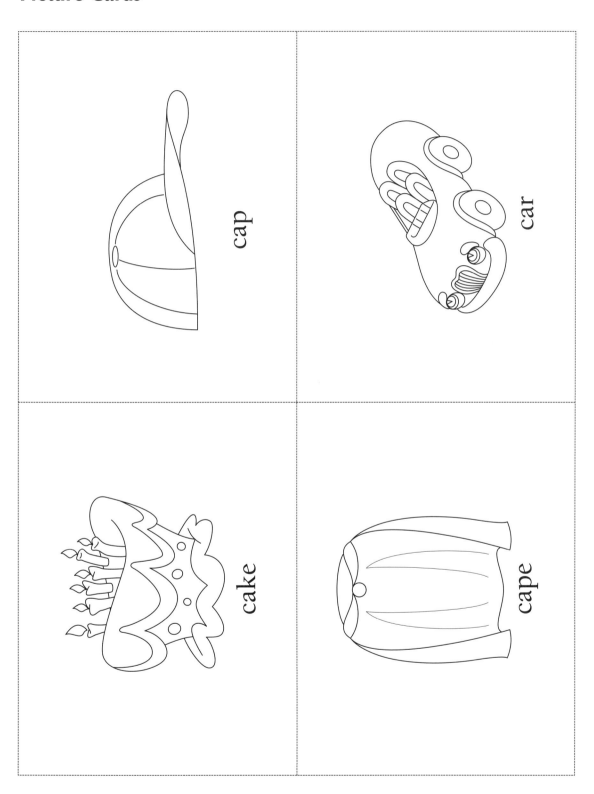

cap

car

cake

cape

Picture Cards

cook

crow

cats

cow

Picture Cards

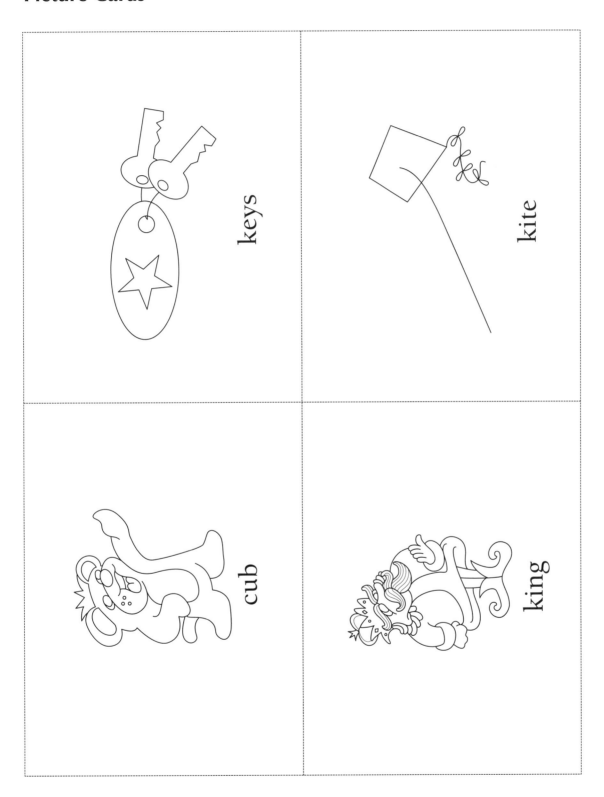

keys

kite

cub

king

Word Count List

Initial /k/	
Word	**Frequency**
cake	2
cakes	2
calico	2
call	2
calls	1
can	1
can't	2
candles	3
candy	1
canes	2
capes	3
caps	1
car	13
carnival	1
cases	1
cats	3
caw	4
coats	4
cold	1
collect	1
come	5
cook	3
cot	1
could	1
counting	1
country	13
counts	1
cows	4
cozy	1
cub	4
cuddle	1
cut	1
ka-boom	1
keep	3
Kelly	2
keys	1
kick	1
kids	1
king	4
Kip	3
kite	2
kites	2

Total Words: 106

Picture Card List

Initial /k/
cake
cap
cape
car
cats
cook
cow
crow
cub
keys
king
kite

Production Practice and Carryover Activities

- Fly **kites**.

- Drive toy **cars**.

- Play charades using **characters** and actions from the story (e.g., **car**, **cook**, **cat**, **cow**, **king**, **kite**).

- Cook a birthday **cake**. **Count** out **candy** pieces and **candles** to decorate it.

- Display pictures of the **cats**, **cow**, and **cub**. Listen to animal sounds on a tape recorder or make sounds live. Have children tell which animal they hear.

- Set up a bean bag **carnival** game. Place target pictures on the floor or on a wall. Hit the pictures with bean bags and name them.

- Eat **candy canes**.

- Draw magic **cars** on paper. Draw or glue pictures of things with the target sound around the **car**. Then tell a story about the things that are seen on a trip in the magic **car**.

- Hide objects that start with the target sound under a **cape** (e.g., **cat** or **cow** figures, toy **car**, **candle**, **candy cane**). Have children feel the object under the **cape** without looking at it and guess what it is.

- Practice putting on and taking off **coats**.

Extension Activities

Rhyming

- Do these words rhyme? (yes or no)

car - bar	cub - cab
count - cot	cake - cook
kiss - keep	key - kite
cast - fast	king - ring
catch - patch	core - more

- Which words rhyme?

kid - hid - keep	candle - kiss - handle
moo - coo - caw	toast - coast - coat
cap - cop - mop	cat - kit - hat
kite - kick - sick	corn - carp - harp
Kelly - cave - wave	keep - kip - peep

- Tell a word that rhymes with *corn, keep, car, cat, king, kite, cot, coast, cake, kick.*

Vocabulary Development

- Read the story and discuss vocabulary that may be new to students: *whoop-ti-doo, calico, crimson, cozy, shed, don, carnival, feast, hit the road, on board.*

Absurdities

- Present illustrations from the story pages or individual sequence cards and talk to students about the absurdities in the pictures. *Do cars really drive all by themselves? Who drives cars? Can cows clap? What can cows do? Who claps? Can cubs fly kites?*

Present Progressive Verbs

- Use the story or sequence cards to elicit present progressive verbs by asking what the different characters are doing: *driving, dancing, clapping, flying kites, counting, licking, cuddling, riding, juggling, raining, playing.*

- Act out actions from the story and have children guess what you are doing.

Sequencing

- Give simple directions for children to sequence pictures along a road. For younger children, use only two or three pictures. Increase the number of pictures according to individual ability levels. Use terms such as *first, second, next,* and *last* to tell the sequence. Have children drive in a pretend car and pick up the various characters. Ask questions about who they are picking up first, second, next, and last.

Critical Thinking

- Show country and city scenes. Discuss how they are the same and different. Ask children where they would rather live and why.

2 Ghosts AND a Goblin

Two ghosts and one goblin,
named Harry, Gus, and Gary,
tried their very hardest
to be extremely scary.

They howled, hooped, hissed, and huffed
like all good ghouls should do.
They moaned, wailed, hid in the dark,
then hopped out with a BOO!

Each time they tried to haunt a house
and give someone a fright,
most folks just gave a chuckle.
Some giggled with delight.

Two ghosts and one goblin,
named Harry, Gus, and Gary,
soon realized they needed help
to be extremely scary.

They hired a witch named Goldie
to get their old BOO! back.
"I'll cast a spell," the old hag wheezed,
"to put you all on track."

4

Goldie grabbed her witch's book
to find a haunting recipe.
"A-HA!" she screamed and hopped right up.
"Here's one I'll guarantee!"

Two ghosts and one goblin
pondered what was next,
for the witch began to dance and chant
and gather up her hex...

"Hocus-pocus, honey locust,
hickory, dickory, plop.
Hair of hamster, halibut,
and great goat-gizzard slop.

Gumdrops, hot dogs, hippo toes,
green gourds, and gardenias.
Howling hounds and coffee grounds,
laughing wild hyenas."

Goldie stirred the mixture up
into a soupy goo,
while Harry, Gus, and Gary
watched her mix the stew.

Goldie soon declared it done,
with hands held high to heaven.
"This spooky spell will take effect
at halfway-past eleven."

So...

Two ghosts and one goblin,
named Harry, Gus, and Gary,
hiked out in the gloomy night,
waiting to be scary.

A haunted house stood still and dark,
and a full moon was peeking.
A hoot owl hooted in a tree,
and a swinging gate was creaking.

Inside a closet crept all three.
Each gave a little smirk.
"Hush," hushed Gus. "It's not quite time
for Goldie's spell to work."

"We mustn't be too hasty.
The clock's just striking seven.
Like Goldie said, we must wait
'til halfway-past eleven."

The two ghosts and one goblin
waited in the dark,
and at halfway-past eleven,
they let the scaring start.

The heavy door heaved open,
and out the three ghouls hopped.
They howled, hooped, hissed, and huffed,
and suddenly—they stopped!

"Ghosts! Goblins!" Gary gasped.
"Let's get out of here!"
Those goofy spooks were frightened
by reflections in a mirror!

The gang of ghouls galloped in horror
but soon slowed to a crawl.
What a silly thing the three had done—
a mirror had scared them all!

Two ghosts and one goblin,
named Harry, Gus, and Gary,
only scared themselves that night
but they'd been scary—VERY!

Sequence Cards

Sequence Cards

Sequence Cards

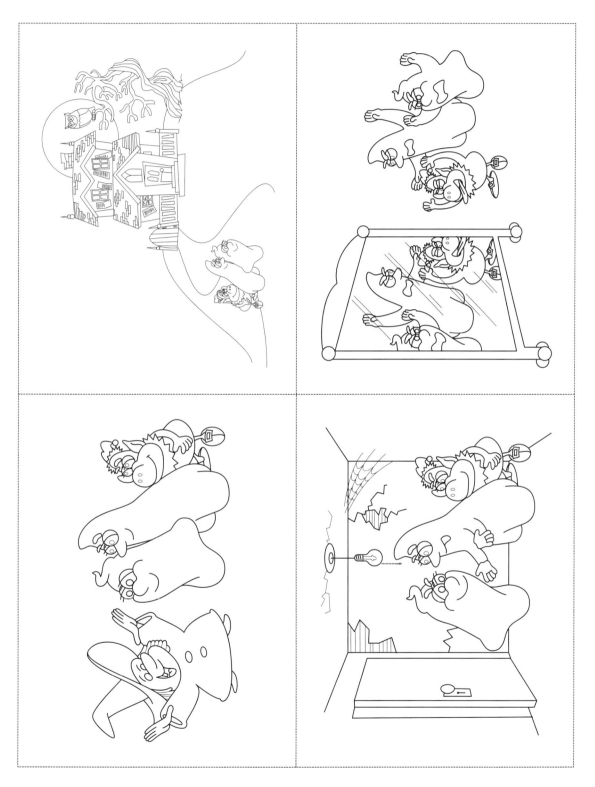

Sequence Cards

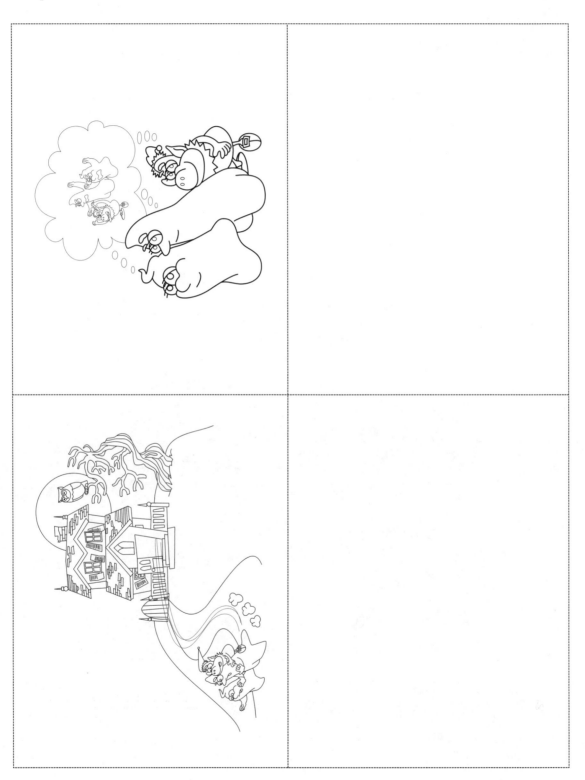

Picture Cards

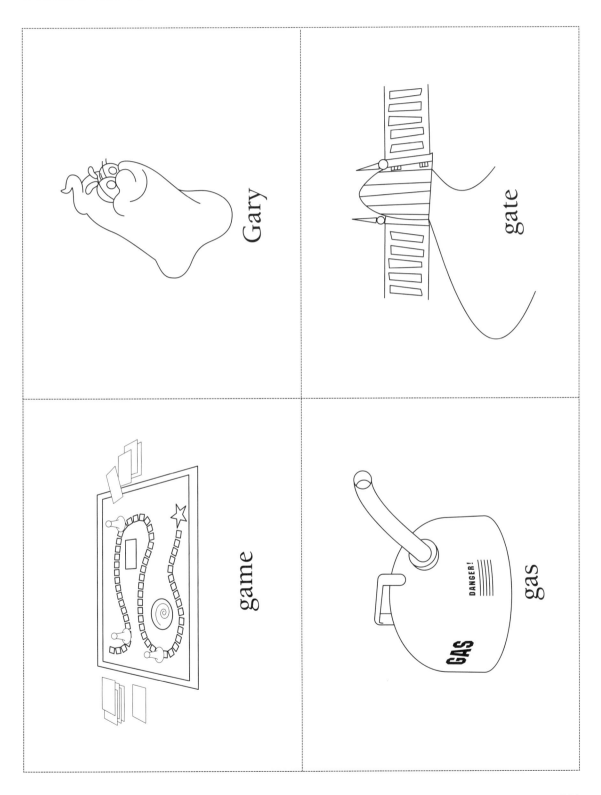

Picture Cards

give

goat

girl

go

Picture Cards

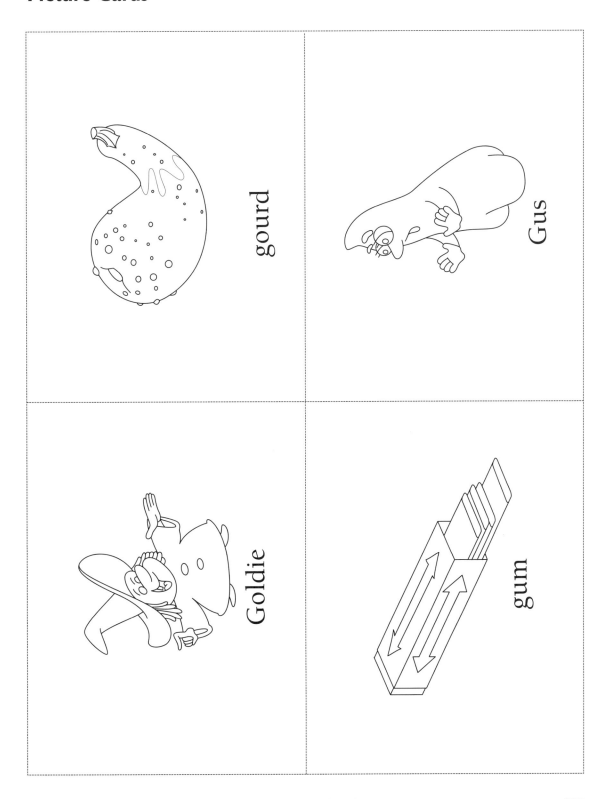

gourd

Gus

Goldie

gum

Picture Cards

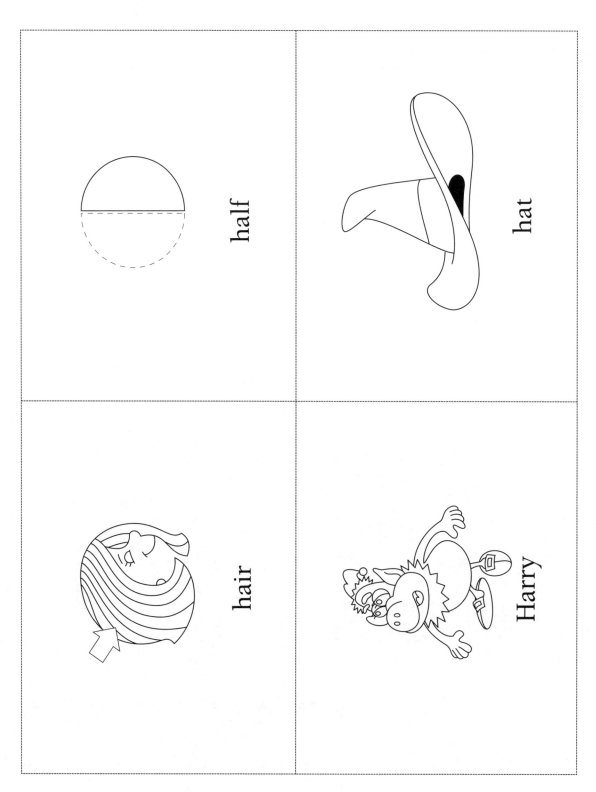

half

hat

hair

Harry

Picture Cards

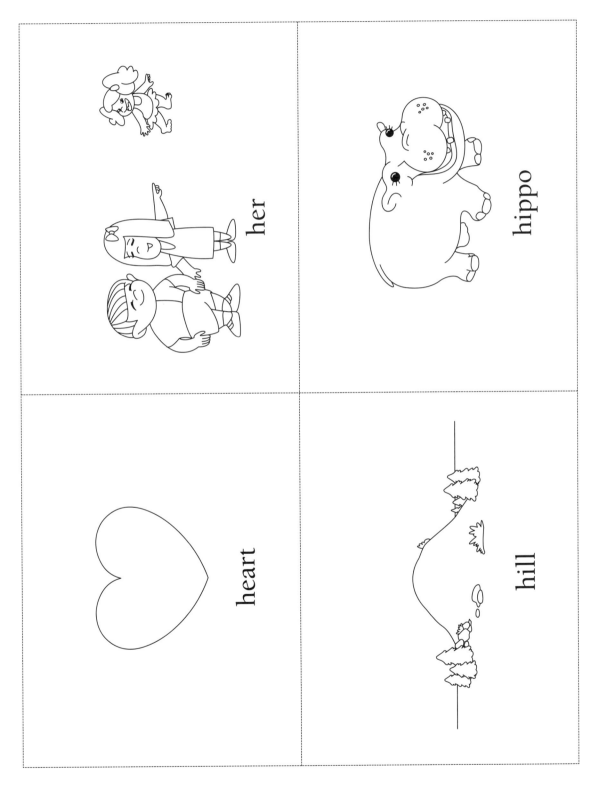

her

hippo

heart

hill

Picture Cards

hot dogs

house

honey

hound

Word Count Lists

Initial /g/		Initial /h/			
Word	Frequency	Word	Frequency	Word	Frequency
galloped	1	had	2	hiked	1
gang	1	hag	1	hippo	1
gardenias	1	hair	1	hired	1
Gary	6	halfway	3	hissed	2
gasped	1	halibut	1	hocus	1
gate	1	hamster	1	honey	1
gather	1	hands	1	hooped	2
gave	2	hardest	1	hoot	1
get	2	Harry	5	hooted	1
ghosts	7	hasty	1	hopped	3
ghouls	3	haunt	1	horror	1
giggled	1	haunted	1	hot dogs	1
give	1	haunting	1	hounds	1
gizzard	1	heaved	1	house	2
goat	1	heaven	1	howled	2
goblin	6	heavy	1	howling	1
goblins	1	held	1	huffed	2
Goldie	5	help	1	hush	1
Goldie's	1	her	3	hushed	1
goo	1	here	1	hyenas	1
good	1	here's	1		
goofy	1	hex	1		
gourds	1	hickory	1		
guarantee	1	hid	1		
gumdrops	1	high	1		
Gus	6				
Total Words: 55		**Total Words: 61**			

Picture Card Lists

Initial /g/		Initial /h/	
game	go	hair	hill
Gary	goat	half	hippo
gas	Goldie	Harry	honey
gate	gourd	hat	hot dogs
girl	gum	heart	hound
give	Gus	her	house

Production Practice and Carryover Activities

- Have children create the outline of a **ghost** using their picture cards. Play music while children **gallop** or **hop** around the pictures. When the music stops, have children name the picture closest to them.

- Make lollipop **ghosts**. Tie white tissue around a lollipop. Use a black marker to draw eyes and a mouth.

- Use markers or paints to decorate **gourds** to look like **ghosts** and **goblins**.

- Use pairs of the pictures and play Go Fish.

- Place objects or pictures with the target sound in **gift** bags. Have children open their **gifts** and tell what they **got**.

- Drive toy cars on a pretend road. Stop at the stoplight and **go** when the light turns green. Stop to **get gas**.

- Show picture cards in front of a mirror and name them. Have children face or **hold** a mirror. Stand behind them and show a picture in the mirror for them to name.

- Take turns making up a **hex** for **Goldie**. Have each child put a specific number of pictures in a bowl. Say "**hocus** pocus" and then name the things they used in their spell.

- Pretend you are **hiding** in a dark closet. Turn off the lights in the room. Use a flashlight to look at and name picture cards.

- Pretend your room is a **haunted house**. Take turns **hiding** cards in the **haunted house** and finding them.

- Cook **hot dogs**. Cut them in **half** before you eat them.

Extension Activities

Rhyming

- Do these words rhyme? (yes or no)

go - no	house - how
Gus - bus	hot - not
give - gave	Harry - Gary
girl - guy	heart - part
game - gold	hag - bag

- Which words rhyme?

Goldie - oldie - girl

most - Gus - ghost

go - game - name

pet - get - gift

wait - gate - white

yell - yelp - help

hocus - pocus - go

clown - honey - funny

hair - head - scare

hide - ride - had

- Tell a word that rhymes with *goo, guy, ghost, guess, go, hound, huff, hair, hoop, hike.*

Vocabulary Development

- Read the story and discuss vocabulary that may be new to students: *hag, recipe, guarantee, reflections, pondered, chant, hex, spell, hired, cast a spell, back on track, take effect.*

Synonyms

- Point out synonyms for several of the vocabulary words: *scream-yell-shout-wail, fright-scare, giggle-chuckle-laugh, stir-mix, smirk-smile-grin, spell-hex-chant, hike-walk, ponder-think.*

Classification

- Present various objects, pictures, and noises. Classify items as being either scary or funny.

Past Tense Verbs

- Use the story or sequence cards and elicit both regular and irregular past tense verbs by asking what the different characters and objects did: *howled, hopped, hissed, huffed, giggled, peeked, hired, wheezed, grabbed, danced, chanted, creaked, hooted, smirked, waited, galloped, hid, crept.*

Critical Thinking

- Create a haunted house. Discuss scary things that would be in a haunted house and what you could use to simulate them. Talk about the sounds you would hear and think of how to create the sound effects.

Notes